CULT LEADERS

CULT LEADERS

THEIR SINISTER TECHNIQUES AND GOALS

AL CIMINO

Al Cimino is a journalist and author who specialises in the genres of true crime and military history. His titles include *War in the Pacific, Nazi Sex Spies, The Mafia, Serial Killers, The Story of the SS* and *21st-Century Psychos.* He lives in London in the UK.

This edition published in 2026 by Arcturus Publishing Limited
26/27 Bickels Yard, 151–153 Bermondsey Street,
London SE1 3HA

AD011077UK
Supplier 40, Date 0326, PI 00011604

Printed in the UK

Authorised Representative:
Easy Access System Europe - Mustamäe tee 50, 10621 Tallinn, Estonia
gpsr.requests@easproject.com

FSC
www.fsc.org
MIX
Paper | Supporting responsible forestry
FSC® C013604

CONTENTS

INTRODUCTION

Weird and wonderful cults have always been with us and some of them have been very nasty indeed. At the end of the third century BC, tree worship came to the Romans in the form of the cult of Cybele, the Great Mother Goddess. Each year, followers cut a pine tree from the forest and erected it in the cult's temple. On the Day of Blood, 24 March, new priests would castrate themselves in front of it. Romans who did so were punished, as if castration was not punishment enough in itself.

Julius Caesar wrote that the Druids made human sacrifices, burning victims alive in a large wooden effigy, sometimes known as a wicker man. This may have been propaganda. The Aztecs were notoriously bloodthirsty, cutting out the hearts of human sacrifices and throwing the bodies of their victims down the stairs of their step pyramids. At the reconsecration of the Great Pyramid of Tenochtitlan, Mexico, it was said that 80,400 were sacrificed over four days, though this was thought by some to have been an overestimate.

The growth of the Abrahamic religions was supposed to have squeezed out cults. However, Christianity was considered to be a cult by the Jews and the Romans. Indeed, it was a pretty bad cult to belong to, given the brutal persecution of the early Church until it was decriminalized by the Edict of Milan in AD 313. It then became the official religion of the Roman Empire. But cults soon appeared within Christianity, which were brutally persecuted by Christians themselves. And there were also those who chose the other side of the Manichaean divide and worshipped Satan – and we know where that leads.

With the waning of Christianity in the face of Darwinism and other scientific advances, new cults sprang up like weeds. The author, G. K. Chesterton, said that if people stop believing in religion, they don't believe in nothing, they believe in everything. Charismatic gurus filled the gap. After all, as L. Ron Hubbard, the founder of Scientology, said: 'If you want to get rich, start a new religion.'

It helps, of course, that religions have tax-exempt status in many countries. Believers are happy to cough up large donations and the gullible are prepared to hand over everything they own and work for free. Then, you can never leave.

If that is not bad enough, you will live in squalor. Absolute obedience is required. There will be brainwashing. Then, the guru will insist on having sex with your spouse and your children. Worse, murder and suicide may also be part of the package.

Thinking of joining up now? Read on and discover just what some cult leaders have inflicted on their followers. And there are many more out there eager to snap up willing recruits. These are just the world's worst cults. So beware.

SEX CULTS

Most cults involve sex in one way or another. It is an important way of keeping control over followers. Even conventional religions impose strict moral codes – sometimes chastity and celibacy. If you can control what people do in the bedroom, you can control the rest of their lives. In cults, recruits can be encouraged to join with the promise of 'free love'. But there tends to be a misogynistic slant, with the female cult members being exploited. Often the cult leader, usually a male, claims the right to have sex with all the women, while denying other men permission. And in the name of sexual liberation, there is paedophilia, with all the damage and misery that causes.

CHAPTER 1:

NXIVM

Modern cults thrive on secrecy, peddling hocus pocus, extorting money from their members and sexual abuse. NXIVM – pronounced 'Nexium' – provided these things in spades, then sued and harassed anyone who criticized them. It ran self-improvement courses using the 'Rational Inquiry' method, which was patented. The methods that it used to shake down its followers amounted to racketeering, with leaders later pleading guilty to that charge.

In a secret subgroup called DOS – Dominus Obsequious Sororium or the 'Lord's Obsequious Sisterhood' – women were enslaved and branded with the leaders' initials. They also had to provide nude pictures or other material that could be used to blackmail them and they had to recruit fresh sex slaves for their master. The cult made no secret of its financial aims or its ambitions of mastery. The cult's name, NXIVM, was based on 'Nexum', a stringent loan contract in early Roman law that left the debtor in bondage to the creditor.

To run such a cult required a charismatic (and unscrupulous) leader. Heading NXIVM was Keith Raniere. Educated in private schools, Raniere would claim in 1989 that he was in the Guinness Book of World Records for 'Highest IQ'. He also claimed to have taught himself high-school maths in 19 hours

Keith Raniere.

when he was 12. That year, he also said he read Isaac Asimov's mind control-themed work, Second Foundation, and credited the novel with inspiring his work in NXIVM. By the following year, he said he had completed three years of college maths and computer-language classes.

He started Consumers' Buyline Inc, which New York State judged to be a pyramid-selling operation. Raniere signed a consent order, admitting no wrongdoing but agreeing to pay a fine.

In 1998, Raniere, along with nurse and would-be therapist Nancy Salzman, founded NXIVM as a 'personal development company' offering Executive Success Programs (ESP) and a range of techniques for self-improvement. These drew on Scientology, Theosophy and neuro-linguistic programming, among other things. They also incorporated elements of multi-level marketing and practices from judo, with bowing and coloured cloth indicating rank.

In the organization, Raniere was 'Vanguard', while Salzman was 'Prefect'. He adopted his pseudonym from his favourite video game, where you gain power from the destruction of your opponents.

They recruited Hollywood actresses and prominent businessmen. It was reported that Richard Branson hosted a VIP session on Necker, his private island in the Caribbean, though Branson denied taking the course.

MONEY, MONEY, MONEY

In 2002, Raniere and Salzman managed to recruit Sara and Clare Bronfman, heirs to the Seagram fortune. Their father, billionaire philanthropist Edgar Bronfman Sr, took a course the following year. Afterwards, he talked to *Forbes* magazine, calling NXIVM 'a cult' and saying that he was troubled about the 'emotional and financial' investment in the operation.

When the article was published, Raniere's former girlfriend, Toni Natalie, contacted Bronfman, warning him that, within a few years, Raniere would be sleeping with both his daughters and that he would also run through their money. After she had split from Raniere, she found that all the debts of the health-food shop they had run together had been put in her name. She filed for bankruptcy and was then subjected to a campaign of harassment.

During her years with Raniere, she became so broken psychologically that, according to court filings, she was persuaded by Raniere to give up the care of her child. With his long brown hair and penetrating blue eyes, Raniere, she said, was 'very charismatic. I mean, he could tell you the sun is purple with pink polka dots and you'd look up and see it.' He was truly brilliant, she said, but in the way 'that brilliance is the closest thing to insanity', recalling how he had insisted she keep the body of her dead puppy in her garage freezer and look at it daily in order to deal with death better.

Nor were his courses entirely safe. In 2003, Kristin Snyder, a 35-year-old environmental consultant, disappeared after a

NXIVM session in Alaska. Her body was never found, but in her truck, parked on the shore of Resurrection Bay, was a note which read: 'I was brainwashed and the emotional centre of my brain was killed/turned off... Please contact my parents... if you find me or this note. I am sorry... I didn't know I was already dead.'

People who survived NXIVM therapy sessions said that they were convinced that they were 'reincarnated Nazis' or 'responsible for 9/11'. Looking back on her experience, Natalie said: 'Keith finds your vulnerabilities and then he preys on them.'

Barbara Bouchey, who ran an asset-management firm, was another of Raniere's girlfriends and a member of the board of NXIVM. Sara and Clare Bronfman became clients and Bouchey arranged a $2 million loan to one of NXIVM's advisors. At

Sara and Clare Bronfman.

Vanguard Week, which celebrated Raniere's birthday, the sisters handed over a giant cardboard cheque for $20 million. They bought a private jet for the cult and covered the losses Raniere made speculating on the commodities markets. He blamed his losses on manipulation by their father. Salzman blew another $70 million; $1.7 million was spent on NXIVM's headquarters and then they began speculating on property in Los Angeles.

The two sisters spent so much that they had to borrow from their father's trust, a sum they did not pay back. The business responsibilities they took on at NXIVM turned out to be a disaster. Lawsuits ensued. Their one success was organizing a visit by the Dalai Lama.

People began to quit NXIVM, demanding $2.1 million (£1.6m) they said was owed to them. Lawyers were hired, costing $1 million (£760,000) a month at one point. Barbara Bouchey, who also quit, was blamed. Sara and Clare Bronfman lost an estimated $150 million (£115m).

Kristin Keeffe, the mother of Raniere's first child, left in 2015, describing Raniere as 'dangerous'. She also claimed that he was blackmailing judges and a senator, and that he had planned to lure his critics to Mexico where they would be convicted on false charges laid before a corrupt judge. Meanwhile, Raniere sued AT&T and Microsoft for patent infringement. The case was thrown out with prejudice when the trial court ruled that he was lying.

SEX TRAFFICKING

In 2017, *The New York Times* began to investigate DOS. Allegations of sexual slavery and financial predation emerged. In March the following year, Raniere was indicted on charges that included sex trafficking, sex trafficking conspiracy and conspiracy to commit forced labour. The following month, Allison Mack, one of the stars of the TV series *Smallville*, was arrested for recruiting for DOS. Clare Bronfman, Nancy Salzman, her daughter, Lauren Salzman, and bookkeeper, Kathy Russell, were also arrested.

Salzman pleaded guilty to a charge of racketeering and criminal conspiracy and, as NXIVM's nominal president, agreed not to contest the forfeiture of the cult's property. She got 42 months, while her daughter got five months' probation after pleading guilty to the same charges. Russell got two years' probation after pleading guilty to visa fraud.

Clare Bronfman pleaded guilty to conspiring to conceal and harbour an undocumented immigrant for financial gain, and fraudulent use of identification and got 81 months in prison. Allison Mack also pleaded guilty to racketeering and racketeering conspiracy and got three years.

On top of racketeering, sex trafficking and conspiracy, Raniere was also charged with possession of child pornography and the sexual exploitation of a 15-year-old girl. He was convicted on all counts and sentenced to 120 years in prison.

CHAPTER 2:

THE COOPERITES

A religious cult, the Cooperites took their name from Neville Cooper, an evangelical preacher who was born in Australia in 1926. A forceful man, he married his wife, Gloria, when she was just 16 because she was passive and compliant.

Cooper preached around Australia, calling his mission 'The Voice of Deliverance'. Those who were saved would enjoy everlasting life in Heaven, while sinners would suffer eternal damnation in Hell. These stern beliefs attracted generous followers. One donated an aeroplane and Cooper became the 'Flying Evangelist'.

Gloria was pregnant with the tenth of their 16 children when the plane's engine cut out. It crashed in a remote area, but those on board miraculously survived for three days in the wild. With no prospect of rescue, Cooper set out to swim a saltwater creek. Exhausted, he reached the far shore and fetched help. Later, he told the *Brisbane Telegraph News Pictorial* that it 'was only God that delivered them from certain death'.

TOTAL SUBMISSION

After taking the word to New Zealand, Cooper and his growing family emigrated there. He set up the Springbank Christian

Church near Christchurch. Emulating the early church, the congregation held their money and possessions in common and formed the Springbank Christian Community. Outsiders wanting to join what became known as Gloriavale underwent an initiation process known as 'submitting', which involved abandoning their careers, opinions, possessions and free will.

Outside contact was forbidden, so they opened a school which concentrated on Bible studies. The community supported the enterprise by farming and running businesses, such as plumbing, drain-laying, gas-fitting, baking, engineering, fixing cars and carpentry. These were run by a group of 16 men who held the dual titles of 'Servants and Shepherds' – the SS.

In 1991, they bought an isolated farm in the bush on the West Coast at the foot of the Southern Alps, which was named after the founder's late wife, Gloria. The community there swelled to 700 and Gloriavale became an economic powerhouse with two large dairy farms, a company exporting sphagnum moss and a helicopter-servicing business.

Cooper changed his name to Hopeful Christian and designed a blue uniform for his followers to wear. The women's dresses were ankle length, so no flesh showed and their hair was hidden under a white cap. Make-up and jewellery were considered ungodly. Even wedding rings were banned as Cooper maintained that they derived from a pagan practice. The outfit inspired the costumes used in Margaret Atwood's dystopian saga, *The Handmaid's Tale*, when it was televised in 2017.

Women were to aspire to be nothing more than homemakers. Abortion, divorce and all forms of contraception were banned. While the women had to submit to the men, the men had to submit to the authority of the church. Absolute obedience was demanded from the children. Every day, school began with Bible reading and prayers. Competitive sport was banned. Pupils were taught that the outside world was evil and they were being saved from its lusts, while discipline was maintained by public beatings.

PHYSICAL ABUSE

Neville Cooper's son Phil, however, was rebellious and he eventually escaped. In his tell-all account, *Sins of the Father*, he said that the older men of the group showed an interest in pornography, and that he had had to endure watching his wife being fondled by his father, while young girls joined community elders in hot tubs.

After Phil fled the compound, he was banned from having any communication with his five children. But in a night-time raid, he rescued them. Later, he freed his wife, but she returned to the community, saying that only by having one of the children's parents stay at Gloriavale would they later be accepted into Heaven.

Worse, Karen Winder, one of Cooper's granddaughters, said that the young men at Gloriavale were 'groomed' to have sex with underage girls.

'These children are growing up in an environment where sex is celebrated,' she said. 'The leader thinks that 13- or 14-year-old girls are ready to have babies.'

She didn't blame them: 'They've grown up sharing a bedroom with their parents – you're there when your parents are having sex. They don't see it as a gross thing.'

There was also physical abuse. One 14-year-old girl was locked in a shack in the bush for four weeks for having an unsanctioned relationship with a boy.

'My dad used to beat us all the time, for no reason,' she said. 'I never knew why. You'd go home and dad would be angry and the first thing he'd do was get a stick and start hitting you.'

'DIRTY OLD MAN'

In 1994, Hopeful Christian was sentenced to six years in prison on 11 charges of indecent assault, but the conviction was overturned on appeal. At a second trial, he was found guilty on three charges of sexual abuse of young community members and spent almost a year in jail. Nevertheless, he returned to head the community while other leaders covered up for him, claiming that he was suffering religious persecution.

In 2017, another of Cooper's granddaughters, Lilia Tarawa, gave a TED talk about the cult, where she said that children were married off to older men at ten or 12. Everyone was made to share everything – from meals to prayers to breastfeeding, with brutal corporal punishment being meted out to people who broke rules. She went on to write *Daughter of Gloriavale: My Life in a Religious Cult*, which was followed by the award-winning TV documentary, *Gloriavale*.

Hopeful Christian, who refused to comment on the fresh allegations, died of cancer in 2018 at the age of 92. He was not missed by former member Yvette Olsen, who said that Christian had sexually assaulted her three times when she was 19. She called him a 'dirty old man' full of 'unbridled lust'.

In 2023, Christian's successor, Howard Temple, was charged with sexual offences against ten girls between 1997 and 2022. The complainants' ages ranged from nine to 20 at the time of the alleged offences. Charges of rape and the sexual abuse of minors have been brought against several other leading members of the Gloriavale community.

The cult has also been charged with the exploitation of workers, violation of employment laws, illegal working conditions and keeping people in servitude. The community's school is also under investigation.

The title of Lilia Tarawa's TED talk said it all: 'I grew up in a cult. It was heaven – and hell.' There was nothing much in between.

Women of the Gloriavale community dressed in conservative clothing. Their outfits were used as the inspiration for the costumes in The Handmaid's Tale TV series.

CHAPTER 3:

CENTREPOINT

Running in parallel with Gloriavale, there was another sex cult in New Zealand. But rather than clothing its nefarious ways in the guise of religion, it openly offered 'sex therapy', often drug-fuelled. Underage children were openly abused, but as with Gloriavale, those ensnared had given up all their possessions in the outside world. There was no escape, so they were forced to turn a blind eye.

Set up in 1978 on a sprawling 30-acre farm near Albany, Centrepoint was modelled on the encounter groups and radical sex therapies popularized in California in the 1960s. Its charismatic leader, Herbert 'Bert' Potter, had built up a following with his therapy workshops, where he gained a reputation for 'unblocking' women who couldn't achieve orgasm. At the height of its popularity, the cult housed around 300 people.

Psychologists flocked to join and counselling services sent women there for daily therapy. Their kids could run free and slept in dormitories, away from their parents. These had toilets with no doors and communal showers, where men came past to watch the naked girls washing themselves.

Potter maintained that there should be no shame and no inhibition. Teenage boys would be taught to perform his techniques on lines of naked adult women. Girls were expected to

Bert Potter.

have sex with adult men from an early age and mothers were encouraged to aid their teenage sons' 'sexual awakening'.

Potter's wife, Margie, held 'education' courses for the teenage girls, and cult members would go off into the bushes to have sex with anyone they chose. This practice was dubbed STT or 'spending time together'.

FORCED INTO SEX

Potter also brought in group drug sessions for all followers over the age of 12, introducing them to MDMA – aka ecstasy – LSD and ketamine.

One of those who suffered was ten-year-old Louise Winn, who had been at the commune for just a month when Margie took her to meet Potter in the first of numerous instances of horrific sex abuse by the couple. First, she had to watch while Potter had sex with his wife, then it was her turn. Early on in her stay, Potter asked her mum Hilary if it was okay to have sex with Louise. When she had threatened him with a knife, she was ordered to undertake more 'therapy'.

Potter wasn't the only one who abused the frightened, little girl. His son, John Potter, followed suit and Dave Mendelssohn, Bert's assistant, also performed sex acts on her. When Louise tried to kill herself, aged 11, Bert told her this was because she wasn't getting 'enough loving', so she was to come to him for sex every day for a week.

Louise sought refuge in one of the caravans on the property, but it had no lock on the door and she would wake in the night to find men in her bed with her. She took to barricading herself in a caravan with piles of junk, to stop other men from climbing into her bed uninvited. She also stopped washing in an attempt to make herself repellent to her abusers.

MIND CONTROL

Researcher Anke Richter believes that parents were brainwashed into ignoring and even participating in their children's abuse.

'Apart from the real sexual predators like Potter and a few others, I don't think the abuse was intentional,' Richter said. 'People were indoctrinated into believing that it's normal for a child to run around naked and if someone touches their genitals it's good for them. They didn't know what we know now – that if a child is hyper-sexualized, it's probably because they have been abused.'

During her research for her book *Cult Trip*, Richter came across Angie Meiklejohn, another Centrepoint survivor. Having moved to the commune with her family, at the age of 14, Angie was groomed, drugged and raped by older men, including Potter, and told Anke she became the 'commune concubine'.

She also had a sexual relationship with Henry Stonex, the therapy group leader who she saw as her 'Centrepoint dad'. His penis was so big it hurt her.

Richter interviewed both victims and abusers.

'The perpetrators I spoke to, including John Potter, said: "Overall, these girls seemed to want it," and some former members still believe that society got it wrong,' she said. 'If you visited Centrepoint, you may have run into a bunch of 13- and 14-year-old, mature-looking, frisky girls who would offer a quickie in the bushes. But that was their survival mechanism in a hierarchical system where you were shamed if you weren't promiscuous as a teenager. I heard one girl described as "a lover of Bert Potter", but she was 13 years old – she was his sexual abuse victim.'

Louise escaped the cult with her mum when she was 14 and later testified against her abusers. In 1992, Potter, then 67, was convicted of 13 charges of indecently assaulting five girls and sentenced to seven years in jail. The judge said he had 'systematically corrupted children for his own sexual pleasure and had abused the power and trust community members placed in him'.

On release Potter – who died in May 2012 – said he still believed that 'intimacy' and 'exploration' between adults and children were natural. Six other male leaders, including Bert's son John Potter and Henry Stonex, were convicted of the sexual assault of a minor.

For the victims, the consequences were lifelong. In an effort to get over the lingering traumas, they turned to drugs, suicide, promiscuity or, in some cases, becoming asexual. Angie Meiklejohn went through addiction and prostitution. Louise Winn couldn't hold down a relationship and was not able to recognize faces because of her trauma.

All this was inflicted on them by people who should have known better – or, at least, always said that they did.

CHAPTER 4:

EASTERN PROMISE

There have been a few scandals surrounding cults that offer enlightenment through various forms of meditation. This began in the 1960s when all things Eastern became trendy through the Maharishi Mahesh Yogi.

Born Mahesh Srivastava in Jabalpur, he claimed to have learnt the basics of his technique, Transcendental Meditation, from spiritual masters in the Himalayas, who made him a Yogi. He took it upon himself to spread its benefits to the world.

In 1975, he established the Maharishi European Research University in Switzerland to conduct research into consciousness. American universities began including TM in their courses. It was practised in jails, factories, farms and offices. Sportsmen, particularly, said they found the technique useful. In some European countries and the Soviet Union, the basics were taught in schools. Soon, the Maharishi became one of the richest men in the world.

He controlled more than 4,000 TM centres in 150 countries, employing over 25,000 teachers. He set up more universities, libraries and presses, whose equipment alone was worth billions. His personal wealth included a large fleet of aeroplanes, helicopters, luxury cars and ships. His British headquarters,

Mentmore Tower in Buckinghamshire, was bought from the Queen for £250 million ($320m).

All sorts of claims have been made for TM. The Maharishi says its purpose is 'to spontaneously unfold the full potential of the individual and thereby to unfold the full potential of every nation'. But more, 'it is a very cosmic design for a global upsurge of orderliness to take the whole human race with all its divergent qualities and values in the direction of happiness and fulfilment.' I leave it to the reader to decide whether the sum total of human happiness and fulfilment has increased a whole lot over the last 60 years.

KRISHNA CONSCIOUSNESS

Following in the footsteps of Transcendental Meditation was Krishna Consciousness. This was the brainchild of Srila Prabhupada. Born in 1896, he was brought up in Calcutta and educated at the Scottish Church College. Both his father and mother worshipped Krishna, the eighth incarnation of the Supreme Being Vishnu. They were strict vegetarians and even abjured tea and coffee. Prabhupada followed in their footsteps.

In the 1920s, there was a revival of the Krishna Consciousness movement in India and Prabhupada was swept along with it. He spent his life translating sacred Hindu texts and writing in English on Hindu thought. He left his wife and, in 1959, became a *sannyasa*, a religious ascetic who relinquishes material things to pursue his faith. In 1965, he sailed to America with a bag full of religious books. In New York, his lectures attracted a small following. Within a year, he had initiated 11 disciples into his order of Krishna Consciousness. They vowed to abstain from alcohol, tobacco, drugs, meat, tea, coffee and sex outside marriage.

CHANTING IN THE STREETS

Prabhupada was an uncompromising guru. Disciples had to renounce all earthly values to follow the spiritual path. Soon his shaven-headed followers in their orange Indian robes became a regular sight dancing and chanting 'Hare Krishna' on the streets of American cities. He founded the International Society for Krishna Consciousness. In 1968, he established ISKCON's headquarters at a country house, bought at a knockdown price from ex-Beatle George Harrison, near Watford in Hertfordshire. By the time of his death in 1977, more than 200 Krishna Consciousness Centres had sprung up around the world.

ISKCON temple, Vrindavan, India.

Before Prabhupada died, he set up the International Governing Body Commission to run the Hare Krishna movement. It comprised 29 of his young followers. However, none of them had the slightest idea how to run the multi-million-dollar empire the swami had bequeathed them. Eleven of them staged a putsch on the unsubstantiated grounds that Prabhupada had authorized their succession on his deathbed. Their leader was Keith Ham, who had taken the name Kirtanananda, and ran things from the New Vrindavan, a temple he had his followers build for him in West Virginia. A British breakaway was run by James Immel, known as Jayatritha.

Without Prabhupada's restraining hand, disciplines began expanding their Krishna Consciousness with LSD. ISKCON came under investigation by anti-cult groups after the parents of two Hare Krishna converts claimed that their children had been brainwashed by the sect. But in a landmark ruling in 1976, the Supreme Court of New York found that Hare Krishna had bona fide religious roots and the children of the converts had freely followed the tenets of their chosen faith. In 1989, a similar case was dismissed by the California court of appeal, although $78,000 damages were awarded over the wrongful death of the 15-year-old's father, who had died, in part, due to the stress of dealing with the Hare Krishnas.

In 1987, Immel was beheaded by his follower John Tiernan, or Navanita Cora, who was probably tripping at the time. Tiernan claimed that he had killed the acid-crazed Immel because he planned to set up his own personal harem among the female devotees, in contravention of the rules laid down by Prabhupada. Tiernan was convicted of murder and committed to a mental institution.

SCHOOLS FOR SCANDAL

In 2002 several of ISKCON's temples filed for Chapter 11, the United States Bankruptcy Code, after a suit for $400m was filed in Texas State Court by victims of abuse, including rape, sexual assault, physical torture and emotional terror, charges alleged to have arisen from behaviour in the temples' schools in the 1970s and 1980s. By the end of the 1970s, the Hare Krishnas were operating 11 schools, known as gurukulas or houses of the guru, in North America, with several more around the world. Most of these closed down in the 1980s.

It was alleged that children at these schools were forced to sleep in unheated rooms and walk great distances in the cold without coats or shoes. They were deprived of medical care for malaria, hepatitis and broken bones, and scrubbed with steel wool until they bled. Some were moved to schools in different states without parental consent.

At a meeting in May 1996, ten former Krishna pupils testified that they had been regularly beaten and caned at school, denied medical care, sexually molested and raped anally at knifepoint.

'I remember being made to sleep naked in a cold bathtub for a month,' said Jahnavi Dasi, who was sent to a Krishna boarding school in Los Angeles at the age of four. 'I had wet my bed, and it was easier for them to make me sleep in the tub than to change my sheets.'

Dasi also told the meeting that she wound up in a diabetic coma for three weeks after her teachers insisted that her health problems were a ruse to avoid cleaning the school and chanting in the temple.

In its own official journal, the Hare Krishna movement published a candid exposé of the widespread physical, emotional and sexual abuse suffered by children sent to live in the group's boarding schools. Parents were often unaware of the abuse because they were busy travelling around soliciting donations for the group, leaving their children in the care of Hare Krishna monks and young devotees who had no training and often resented the task, the report said.

'We need to get to the bottom of it,' Anuttama Dasa, the North American director of communications for ISKCON, said, 'and to the best of our ability do whatever we can to try to repair the damage to the kids and show them we do care as a religious society.'

LORD OF THE NIGHT

The most notorious of the new-style Indian swamis was Bhagwan Shree Rajneesh, which means 'Holy Glorious Lord of Darkness'. Born Chandra Mohan Jain to a wealthy middle-class family, he was brought up by his grandparents who spoiled him. Rajneesh was a childhood nickname meaning 'Lord of the Night'.

He became an honours student at the University of Jabalpur, where he went on to become Professor of Philosophy. In 1966, he quit, claiming that he had attained enlightenment without the help of a guru or any rigorous religious discipline. He invented 'dynamic meditation' which involves catharsis – usually in the form of expressions of anger or sexual intercourse. This was one of the many forms of meditation he came up with in his lifetime.

Bhagwan Shree Rajneesh.

In 1969, he moved his centre of operations to Bombay, now Mumbai, where he was besieged by young Western drop-outs searching for enlightenment. He took them on as his pupils and, in exchange for everything they owned, he gave them lectures and rose-coloured robes. They were encouraged to chant mantras, kick, bite, scream and punch to release pent-up emotions, romp naked and have as much sex as they could manage. Rajneesh took the title Bhagwan – which means 'Master of the Vagina' – and maintained his state of enlightenment with a string of young female initiates, some of whose seduction was little short of rape as the guru took it upon himself to teach them the spiritual benefits of sexual submission.

Nude romps on the beach under the auspices of the Bhagwan attracted the hostility of the locals, so the cult moved to Poona, aka Pune. To support the ashram, the Bhagwan's followers took to smuggling drugs. When a BBC documentary exposed this, the Indian authorities began an investigation. Fleeing charges of fraud and tax evasion, the Bhagwan moved his operations to Antelope, a small town in Wasco County, Oregon, where he bought a desert property called Big Muddy Ranch for $6 million (£4.7m) and renamed it Rajneeshpuram.

LIFE OF LUXURY

While his followers toiled there in squalor, the Bhagwan lived in luxury. He had four private aircraft, a private arsenal, an endless supply of submissive young women and 93 Rolls-Royces, using a different one every day for drive-by ceremonies, his only interaction with devotees. For them, the regime grew stricter. Under the cosh of the cult's police force, all elements of individuality were stamped out and the outside world, including friends and family, was dismissed as worthless and meaningless.

Cult members infiltrated the local council and effectively took over the town. Buildings were erected on the ranch without planning permission and, when state officials protested, their offices were firebombed. The ensuing Federal investigation discovered laboratories containing chemical and biological agents at the ashram. The Bhagwan turned against senior lieutenants, including his chief of staff and president of Rajneesh Foundation International, Ma

Rajneeshpuram, the small town in Oregon that was home to the Rajneesh movement in the 1980s.

Anand Sheela, aka Sheela Patel, and shopped them to the authorities. Threatened with prosecution for immigration violations and in fear of an assault on his compound by the National Guard, he organized a human shield of his concubines and children. In the end, he fled.

He headed for Bermuda, but when his private jet set down at Charlotte-Douglas International Airport in Carolina to refuel, he was arrested and taken to jail in chains. Convicted of making false visa applications, he was fined $400,000 and deported. However, India refused him residence. He headed to Nepal, then hopped around the globe for two years, after being refused entry to 21 countries. In 1987, the Indian government finally let him settle back in Poona.

WHERE WE ARE NOW

At the height of his career, the Bhagwan had 600 meditation centres around the world. Only 20 were left when he died. The cult, which now operates under the name Osho, was taken over by Canadian real estate magnate, Michael William O'Byrne, known to the devout as Swami Prem Jayesh. His slimmed-down operation still nets some $45 million (£35m) a year 'de-stressing' business executives. Two followers, Sally-Anne Croft or Ma Prem Savita, and Susan Hagan or Ma Anand Su were extradited from England back to Oregon in 1995 for conspiring to murder a lawyer who had been investigating the cult's salmonella attack on the salad bars in ten restaurants nearby in an attempt to influence local elections, poisoning 751. They were convicted and sentenced to five years' imprisonment.

Followers still proselytize the Bhagwan's Mystic Rose Meditation, which the Bhagwan claimed was 'the greatest breakthrough in meditation in 2,500 years' and, of all the meditations he had invented, 'perhaps the most essential and fundamental one'.

CHAPTER 5:

JESUS FREAKS

In 1966, Frank Zappa and the Mothers of Invention were urging everyone to 'freak out' with the album *Freak Out!* So was Tom Wolfe in his book, *The Electric Kool-Aid Acid Test*, in 1968. This movement involved loud rock music and hallucinogenic drugs. But some evangelical Christian preachers realized that young people could be made to freak out on Jesus as well.

One of them was David Berg. At first sight he appeared an unpromising figure. A former Methodist minister, he was middle-aged, pot-bellied and balding. His early childhood was spent touring around the country with his evangelist parents who preached at revival meetings. After being drummed out of various sects, they settled in Miami.

Graduating from high school, he went to business school. Then, he became a minister but was dismissed from a church in Arizona, allegedly for sexual misconduct with an employee, though he claimed it was for encouraging greater racial divergency in his congregation. Then in 1968, he turned up in California when the hippie movement was in full swing.

He managed to attract a bunch of kids who congregated along the beaches of California to a club Berg called Teens for Christ. There, Father David, aka Moses, delivered traditional evangelical teaching dressed up in the language of sex, drugs and rock'n'roll, while Berg's wife Jane, or 'Mother Eve', dished out peanut butter sandwiches. Many of Berg's young recruits had abandoned their jobs and families to drop out of 'straight' life. They were attracted by free food and, possibly, Berg's anti-establishment view of the meaning of life.

ANYTHING GOES

A journalist dubbed Berg's followers the 'Children of God'. Berg adopted the title in his fledgling career as a tele-evangelist, appealing particularly to the young. The cult became hip when Jeremy Spencer, guitarist of Fleetwood Mac, quit the band mid-tour to join the Children of God. Nevertheless, those square enough to embrace Christianity were dismissed as 'Jesus Freaks', a soubriquet Berg's followers sought to embrace.

Originally, Berg had preached the joys of celibacy. But when an attractive new young female recruit named Karen 'Maria' Zerby joined the cult, Berg began preaching the joys of free love. He declared that Karen was his second wife, though Jane stayed on in the cult. He also 'shared' the wives of other cult members. In 1970, he divorced Jane and married Karen, adopting her son, Ricky Rodriguez.

Berg preached that, as God is Love, anything goes sexually – including incest, homosexuality and paedophilia. But when the allegations of the sexual abuse of the cults' children surfaced, Berg back-pedalled on paedophilia, declaring it an excommunicable offence. Nevertheless, sexually suggestive photographs of Rodriguez with adult caretakers appeared in the cult's childrearing handbook.

Recruits had to give everything they owned to the cult. If they left, they would give up any hope of salvation. Children of God (COG) were expected to cut off all ties with their friends and families outside the cult, but, in 1972, FREECOG was set up to help parents reclaim their children from the cult. It was the first of the modern anti-cult organizations that kidnapped cult members and subjected them to intensive anti-brainwashing techniques. The cult was also under investigation by the authorities, so Berg decamped to England, setting up his new headquarters in Bromley, Kent.

OUT OF CONTROL

The Children of God spread widely throughout the world, but Berg feared that the cult was slipping beyond his control. Leaders in individual countries were taking too much authority to themselves. In 1978, he dismissed over 300 of them, including his own daughter and her husband, who were COG leaders in South America. In all, 2,600 members were culled, a third of the world membership. Those that remained were invited to join Berg's new brainchild, the Family of Love, which, chillingly, began calling itself The Family.

To increase membership, Berg introduced Flirty Fishing or FFing. The idea came from Karen who had been recruiting new men by taking them to bed for years. Christ was a fisher of men and, Berg said, to fish you need bait, so he sent out young attractive female cult members – married and single – to pick up men in bars and clubs. Once bedded, they would be lured into the fold. In the 1980s, the fear of AIDS put a stop to FFing. It is not known how effective a recruiting method it was. Some say it brought more women into the cult than men.

Sexual freedom has since been confined to those within the cult and was not extended to new recruits until they had completed a six-month probationary period. Children of God lived a communal life, supported by donations and sales of their posters, music and videos. Sometimes cult members took on regular jobs if more income was needed.

By and large, The Family did not look after its members well. Of the 1,000 members recruited in the south of England, at least 116 died over a ten-year period. The police were on the case. When prosecutions began in 1994, Berg disappeared and died in Portugal later that year. Berg's second wife, Maria – aka Mama Maria – took over.

'HELL ON EARTH'

In November 1995, in England's High Court, Lord Justice Ward declared that Berg was sexually depraved and the cult had not forsworn paedophilia at all. However, he ruled that a 28-year-old member could keep her three-year-old son – over the protests of the child's grandmother – provided she renounce the teachings of David Berg. A Love Charter outlawed some of the cult's more abusive practices. There were investigations into The Family for child abuse and prostitution in Argentina, France, Spain, Australia, Venezuela and Peru.

In 2004, The Family became The Family International. Members were encouraged to have a sexual relationship with Jesus in the imagination. Men were encouraged to think of themselves as women to prevent risking a homosexual relationship with the Son of God.

Berg's granddaughter fled the cult after being sexually abused as a child. Some of the abusers have been prosecuted and others who escaped said that living in the cult was 'Hell on Earth'. In January 2005, Ricky Rodriguez murdered one of the female caretakers shown in the handbook before taking his own life several hours later.

THE JESUS ARMY

Another group of Jesus Freaks that took root in Britain was the Jesus Army, aka the Jesus Fellowship Trust. This began in 1967, when Baptist minister, Noel Stanton, and some members of his church in Bugbrooke, Northampton, started speaking in tongues. They began healing and preaching the gospel in the new hippie jargon of the 'Jesus Revolution'.

The message was straightforward evangelical Christianity but preached with theatrical flair. Stanton condemned sports, drinking and 'worldly music', and he took a hammer to guitars, videos and music cassettes.

Soon his church was too small for the burgeoning congregation it attracted. Stanton raised donations and bought buildings to house his community, supported by the produce of its New Creation Farm.

A Jesus Army open-air ceremony in London, 2010.

Communal houses spread across the UK. The Jesus Army wore camouflage jackets, combat gear and army boots. Bussed around in brightly painted 'Battle Busses', they ran health-food shops, builders, plumbers and a clothes store.

In the communal houses, everything was shared, including money and clothes. TV and radio were banned, along with most newspapers. Only religious music was played. The Jesus Army did not even celebrate Christian festivals such as Christmas on the grounds that they have their origins in paganism.

Sex was actively discouraged. Even long-married couples had to sleep in separate beds. Romantic liaisons between members required the permission of the leadership and traditional gender roles were strictly observed.

Recruits had to hand over everything they owned to the Army. However, the Jesus Army said they kept members' money in a trust fund, which would be handed back to them if they decided to leave.

After Noel Stanton's death in 2009, the Jesus Amy itself supplied allegations to Northamptonshire Police of sexual offences against Stanton and others, and as of 2019 there were 43 complaints of historic sexual and physical abuse, largely against children.

The Jesus Fellowship Redress Scheme was set up to compensate members who had suffered. It identified 539 alleged perpetrators of alleged abuse, many of them the leaders. So far, 601 individuals have applied for damages, though the true number of victims was probably greater. Twelve former members of the Jesus Fellowship Church have been convicted of indecent assaults and other offences.

In October 2021, the variously named Jesus Army, Jesus Fellowship Church, Jesus Centres Trust changed its name to the JCT – Jesus Fellowship Communities Together Limited.

CHAPTER 6:

THE SCIENCE RESEARCH FOUNDATION

In 2007, thousands of scientists, universities and schools around the world received an unsolicited – and in most cases unwanted – present. It was an 800-page, glossily illustrated book, weighing 12 lb (5 kg), called *The Atlas of Creation*. It was written by Harun Yahya, the pseudonym of Turkish author Adnan Oktar and founder of the Science Research Foundation, which sought to refute Darwinism and which propounded various conspiracy theories in the attempt to do so.

Although he purported to be a feminist, Yahya's TV show featured a bevy of pneumatic would-be Barbie Dolls known as 'kittens', who all wore heavy make-up, had bleached-blond hair and had undergone plastic surgery, so that they looked astonishingly alike. They also all happened to be wealthy socialites.

ZEALOT

Born in Ankara in 1956, Adnan Oktar read the books of the dissident Muslim theologian, Said Nursi, as a child and became a Sunni zealot. He studied at Mimar Sinan University in

Istanbul, which was, at the time, dominated by Marxists and other left-wingers. He collected around him others who were interested in religion and attacked Marxism and materialism in general. In his pamphlet, 'The Theory of Evolution', he insisted that Darwinism was un-Islamic because it contradicted the creationism found in the Koran. Fellow Islamic scholar Edip Yüksel broke with him when it became clear that Oktar believed he was the Mahdi – that is, the redeemer of Islam, who is said to be going to appear before the Day of Judgement. One supposed incarnation of the Mahdi was Muhammad Ahmad, who killed General Gordon at Khartoum.

Unlike the clean-shaven Said Nursi and Edip Yüksel, Oktar grew a beard. But it was not the long raggedy beard favoured by most Islamic fundamentalists. He kept his beard neatly trimmed and always appeared stylishly dressed. His aim was to attract the children of the rich.

Oktar also attracted the attention of the media, even appearing on the front cover of the leading Turkish political weekly *Nokta*. In 1986, he published a 550-page book called *Judaism and Freemasonry*, where he contended that Zionists and Masons had a covert influence on the government, universities, political parties and the press.

'The principal mission of Jews and Freemasons in Turkey was to erode the spiritual, religious, and moral values of the Turkish people and make them like animals,' he wrote. 'I want to resemble Prophet Solomon. Prophet Solomon was like this. He used to be well dressed. He liked being well dressed. His palace was beautiful; there were beautiful people around him. Allah is beautiful. Allah loves those who are beautiful, wants everywhere to be beautiful. Paradise is also beautiful. [The] aim of a Muslim should be beauty.'

The stylishly dressed Adnan Oktar, leader of the Science Research Foundation.

MENTAL ILLNESS?

He was arrested and charged with promoting a theocratic revolution. This was outlawed under Turkey's secular constitution. Although he was never formally charged, he served 19 months, at first confined to a medical wing. Then, he was diagnosed with an obsessive-compulsive personality disorder and schizophrenia and sent to a mental hospital. Colleague-turned-critic Edip Yüksel, who was in prison at the same time, believed that he was faking his symptoms to avoid compulsory military service.

'It was ironic, since he was indeed mentally sick,' said Yüksel. 'He was a delusional megalomaniac, yet he was cunningly acting out another mental illness.'

Back at large, Oktar built up a community of followers, recruiting them in the swanky summer resorts along the shores of the Sea of Marmara. In 1990, he established the Science Research Foundation (in Turkish, the *Bilim Araştırma Vakfı*, or BAV). He specialized in enlisting good-looking boys as they would then attract pretty girls. Though professing to be a good Muslim, he followed in the ways of Christian cult leaders.

'Knowing him before the 1990s, I could not believe that he would be indulging in promiscuous sexual activities,' wrote Yüksel. 'He would not even shake hands with women. However, with time, Adnan evolved and transformed. His sexual abuse of girls around him has been a frequent topic in the Turkish media and acknowledged by the defectors. He claims the right to have sexual intercourse with every female member of his cult. He has even invented a name for those females: MOTOR (engine). Reportedly, his male followers are feeling lucky in letting him taste [*sic*] their girlfriends first.'

A defector from the cult named Berk, who had spent seven years with them, said: 'There were sisters, concubines and brothers, the male members. The brothers were allowed to marry the concubines, while the sisters were all married to Adnan Hodja – that is, Adnan "the Teacher".'

'Everyone had to be the same,' Berk told *New Humanist* magazine. 'The hairstyle, the shoes, the jackets. It had to be the most expensive brands, like Versace and Gucci, and it had to be exactly how he wanted it to be. Even our communal flats had to be furnished according to his taste.'

SEX SLAVES

Again, there was a tinge of paranoia around his behaviour. The article went on: 'Video cameras were installed in the communal apartments, which allowed Oktar to exercise control over his followers and outsiders... young girls were lured into sex parties with the promise of being admitted to the group but ended up having to perform sexual acts with men of influence, whom the group needed for its economic and political success. The encounters were filmed and used to coerce the men in question to act in the group's interest.'

Others said that members of the group treated the women as their 'sex slaves', with Oktar and his followers coercing them into performing oral sex and other sexual favours. Oktar justified this concubinage by citing Ottoman harems, while passages of the Koran were used to justify his practice of forcing his young followers to sever ties with their families. According to Oktar, love for one's mother and father was an offence against God. Parents were seen as the executors of God's will in raising children, but once a child had grown up their role was finished.

BROUGHT TO JUSTICE

After local elections in 1994, Recep Tayyip Erdoğan was elected as Mayor of Istanbul (before going on to become prime minister, and then president, of Turkey). Erdoğan needed Islamist support and Oktar, with his well-resourced social network, was a valuable ally. However, despite his growing political influence, in 1999 Oktar was arrested and sentenced to three years in prison for creating an illegal organization for personal gain. Oktar successfully appealed against the charge and it was eventually dropped in 2010.

He then served as an adviser to several Turkish politicians, and received endorsements from Arab countries, including Saudi Arabia and Dubai, where his publishing empire flourished. He also courted the Western media, offering journalists all-expenses-paid flights to Istanbul to anybody wishing to interview him.

His anti-Darwinism has won him the endorsement of conservative Congressmen in the US. He also defended his reputation at home by taking out numerous libel suits against people who criticized him on websites. Meanwhile, on his TV talk show with his 'kittens', he has discussed Islam and shown fossils that supposedly discredit Darwinian evolution.

In July 2018, Oktar and over 160 of his associates were arrested and charged with running a criminal organization, having sexual intercourse with minors, kidnapping children, sexual harassment, blackmail, wrongful imprisonment, political and military espionage, fraud by exploiting religious feelings and beliefs, money laundering, violation of privacy, forgery of official documents, opposition to anti-terror law, coercion, slander, alienating citizens from mandatory military service, insulting behaviour, false incrimination, perjury, aggravated fraud, opposition to the law against smuggling, opposition to tax laws, bribery, depriving others of the right to education and civil rights, torture, illegal recording of personal data and violating the law on the protection of the family and of women. He condemned this as a British plot.

In 2021 Oktar was convicted and sentenced to 1,075 years in prison. The verdict was overturned on appeal. At a retrial, the following year, the sentence was increased to 8,658 years.

DEATH CULTS

Some cults openly condone murder, while others encourage or even coerce their followers into committing suicide on the misguided premise that they are going to a better place. But then there are some cult leaders who are so reckless with the lives of others that they deliberately put their followers in harm's way. Many cults are hedged around with paranoia, the belief that the authorities or society as a whole are out to get them. To prove that they were right all along, they provoke the police or the government into taking action. It never turns out well.

CHAPTER 7:

AUM SHINRIKYO

Early on the morning of 20 March 1995, five members of the Aum Shinrikyo 'Supreme Truth' cult got on five different trains at the extremities of three lines of the Tokyo subway system. At 8.15am, the height of the city's morning rush hour, these trains would converge on the Kasumigaseki, the centre of Japan's national government. Four or five stations before, the five cult members surreptitiously dropped vinyl bags they had been concealing behind newspapers. With the sharpened tip of umbrellas, they pierced the bags. Then, they slipped off the train and disappeared into the crowds on the platform.

As the packed trains headed on towards their destinations, a solution of 30 per cent sarin leaked out of the bags. Sarin is a nerve agent developed by the Nazis, though not used. It is a colourless, tasteless, odourless gas that can kill any living being within 100 feet in a matter of minutes. Soon, the deadly gas was rising around the ankles of the commuters.

Aum Shinrikyo's leader, Shoko Asahara, had ordered the gas attack. His aim was to paralyze the government of Japan, as a first step in his plan for world domination. It failed, but 13 innocent people died, and the attack injured another 50, causing temporary vision problems for a further 1,000.

CRAZY MAN OR VISIONARY?

It is easy to dismiss Shoko Asahara as a madman. He was a half-blind, overweight hippie conman and murderer who admired Adolf Hitler and believed that he was the reincarnation of Imhotep, the Egyptian architect who built Egypt's first pyramid in the 27th century BC. Although there is no evidence that he was a physician, Imhotep became associated with the Greek god of medicine and a cult grew up around him that survived well into Roman times.

At the time of the Tokyo atrocity, Asahara was 41 and had built up a following of between 3,000 and 10,000. They were not the deadbeats picked up off the street that many cults depend on. The assassins he deployed on the subway trains were: Ikuo Hayashi, a 48-year-old cardiovascular surgeon who had studied in the US before working as head of Circulatory Medicine at the National Sanatorium Hospital and joining Aum; 37-year-old Yasuo Hayashi, an electronics engineer who had studied artificial intelligence; 31-year-old Masato Yokoyama, an applied physics graduate working for an electronics firm; 30-year-old physicist Kenichi Hirose, who had published a paper on high-temperature superconductivity before joining Aum; and 27-year-old Toru Toyoda, a graduate student in physics who was about to start a doctorate at Tokyo University before dropping out to follow Asahara.

Their leader's education was slight by comparison. Born the fourth son of a weaver of the straw mats used as flooring in Japanese homes, he had been educated at a school for the blind. Then plain Chizuo Matsumoto, he suffered from infantile glaucoma and was blind in the left eye and partially sighted in the right. Having some sight gave him a tremendous advantage over the other pupils, whom he bullied, extorting money from them. By the time he left high school, he had amassed £20,000 ($26,000).

He aspired to be prime minister and applied to study politics at Tokyo University but failed the entrance exam. Instead, he studied acupuncture and opened a traditional Chinese shop outside Tokyo. The following year, he met a pretty college-educated girl called Tomoko. They married in January 1978. Six months later, the first of their six children was born.

With money from Tomoko's family, Chizuo set up the Matsumoto Acupuncture Clinic. It prospered and Chizuo branched out into quack remedies. He began marketing what he called Almighty Medicine at £5,000 ($6,500) for a three-week course. The Medicine proved to be merely tangerine peel doused in alcohol. He was arrested for practising pharmacy without a licence and selling unregulated drugs.

BIZARRE EXPERIMENTS

Like many other young people who had grown up in Japan's booming post-war economy, he was searching for a more spiritual dimension to life. He let his hair and beard grow. Adopting the name Shoko Asahara, he began taking an interest in all forms of mysticism from fortune-telling to geomancy, and began bizarre experiments that, he believed, gave him the power to read other people's auras.

He joined a religious cult called Agon Shu. A fundamentalist Buddhist sect, Agon Shu had its own satellite TV station, which it used, it said, to beam out 'healing power'. Followers could develop their psychic powers, provided they cut all contact with their families.

Asahara then embarked on his own spiritual voyage. He meditated for 40 minutes a day for 1,000 days... and emerged enlightened. He made several trips to India where he set off to the Himalayas to walk the same path as Buddha and met the Dalai Lama.

In 1984, he registered Aum Inc. – Aum after the Hindu mantra 'om' – and opened his own one-room yoga school, where he sold his own patent medicines as a sideline. It was called the Aum Association of Immortal Mountain Wizards. He also claimed to have discovered visionary powers, which enabled him to read people's minds and see their past lives. In the future, he believed, he would be able to fly.

Asahara preaches to his followers.

ON THE UP

He told the cult magazine, *Twilight Zone*, that he was a messiah and claimed that he could levitate for three seconds, though his flight capability was increasing all the time. In fact, his levitation was simply a yoga trick performed by bouncing, but a photographer managed to catch him mid-hover. The magazine ran the picture and his yoga school rocketed in popularity. Soon, he was opening a chain of schools across Japan.

Up until this point, Asahara was merely a cheap conman, but then a dark side began to emerge. He claimed that a mystic he had met in the mountains told him that Armageddon was coming at the end of the 20th century. Then, while meditating, a voice had come to him, telling him that God had chosen him to be the leader of God's army.

He began writing books. The first was called *Secrets of Developing Your Supernatural Powers*. In it, the 'Venerable Master' claimed to be able to teach mind-reading, how to travel into the fourth dimension, develop X-ray vision and levitate. Asahara put the *Twilight Zone's* picture of him levitating on the cover to prove the point. The blurb read: 'Spiritual training that doesn't lead to supernatural powers is hogwash!'

The book brought in a flood of new followers, so Asahara supercharged his whole operation. The Aum Association of Immortal Mountain Wizards became Aum Supreme Truth. Instead of three-day yoga courses costing £25 ($33), the great guru would now inject 'divine energy' directly into a follower's head for £250 ($330). Spiritual development now came from straightforward cash donations and devotees were expected to distribute leaflets advertising Asahara's books.

The central tenet of the cult was now the forthcoming Apocalypse, borrowing from Nostra-damus, the Christian Armageddon, the Hindu god of destruction Shivas and the idea in Japanese Buddhism of *mappo* – the age of degeneration and chaos.

According to Asahara, Japan would re-arm in 1992, precipitating World War III. The ensuing nuclear holocaust would destroy the world in 2003. This could be prevented if those enlightened by his teachings took over in every country. This was detailed in his book, *Day of Annihilation*. Even if it did happen, it didn't matter. Those he had enlightened would emerge from the destruction as a post-holocaust race of superhumans. Asahara had already developed superpowers himself, claiming to be able to meditate underwater, without breathing, for an hour – though he forgot to call the *Guinness Book of World Records*.

THE COST OF ENLIGHTENMENT

Marketing went into overdrive with advertisements in magazines, mailshots and telephone campaigns. Recruits were invited to come to 'Truth Meetings' where they were treated to videos of Asahara and told that they had been initiates in a previous life.

Locks of Asahara's hair were boiled up to make tea and drunk, or initiates were told to drink Asahara's blood and semen. They were then enrolled on expensive courses designed to raise them to new levels of consciousness. Enlightenment never comes cheap.

In Aum's US branch, followers simply had to cleanse themselves by donating large amounts of money. Further funds were raised by selling Asahara's beard clippings or his dirty bathwater, which he called 'Miracle Pond'. Demand soon outstripped supply, so Aum sold straight tap water, called 'Nectar Water', which Asahara had transformed into a mysterious fluid that emitted light as he explained in his book, *Declaring Myself Christ*. Naturally, it cost much more than regular water.

In 1988, Aum's headquarters moved into a compound on the slopes of Mount Fuji. Followers paid £1,250 ($1,600) for week-long seminars there. They slept on the floor, ate one bowl of boiled vegetables a day and drank filthy stagnant water that had been blessed by Asahara. The rotund guru himself did not share this spartan regimen, keeping up his strength on massive meals of the finest foods.

Devotees had to cut their ties with their families. They had to surrender everything they owned and were cut off from the outside world. Given new names, they were deprived of sleep, a condition that made them highly suggestible. Asahara admitted using brainwashing techniques, but then he was 'spiritual dictator of the world'.

INHUMAN TREATMENT

Children born within the Aum compound were not given names, rather a designation letter. They were left to their own devices in squalid conditions and were given no formal education, except being taught to admire Asahara's own idol – Adolf Hitler.

The smallest act of disobedience would be punished with a savage beating. Or offenders could be locked in tiny cells with a video of Asahara played at maximum volume, 24 hours a day. Otherwise, they would find themselves in solitary confinement in pitch darkness and be forced to fast for a week. Children as young as ten were punished in this way.

Devotees were forbidden to have sex. Anyone who did was forced to wear a dog collar and beg for scraps, or be hung by the feet at the Master's pleasure. Strangely, this did not seem to put anyone off and Asahara invested his profits on Tokyo's buoyant stock exchange. At the same time, he applied to get Aum Supreme Truth tax exemptions as a religious organization. This was opposed by the parents of his followers, who claimed the cult had robbed them of their children.

Asahara responded with lawsuits and the harassment of government officials. When the authorities capitulated and gave Aum its tax exemption, the press tried to take him on. Taro Maki, the editor of *Sunday Mainichi*, ran a series of exposés on Aum and Asahara. Asahara hit back with the book, *The Insanity of the Sunday Mainichi: Taro Maki's Ambitions*. *Mainichi's* offices and the neighbourhood around Maki's home were plastered with fliers defaming him and his family were harassed by late-night phone calls. But the police were loath to act. Buddhism had been suppressed by the hardline militarist government before World War II and any move against a quasi-Buddhist organization might be seen as a return to the bad old days.

MIND-READER

Asahara claimed that Aum was the fastest-growing religion in the history of Japan. Young people were attracted as the cult's stern discipline emulated the rigid school system they had been used to. And Asahara's apocalyptic vision echoed the fantasy world they knew from computer games, cartoons, ultra-violent comics and *Godzilla*.

Young scientists dropped out of university to join Aum, which offered some spiritual succour beyond the rigid materialism they had been taught. Hideo Murai, who had a PhD in astrophysics and computer programming, quit the R&D department at Kobe Steel to become Aum's chief scientist because he saw parallels between Aum and Isaac Asimov's *Foundation* series.

Asahara himself had a strange relationship with science. He had been hooked up to a faulty EEG machine and shown to be 'brain dead' – that is, the machine registered little or no brain activity. For Asahara, this was a good thing. With no brainwaves of his own, he said he could pick up other peoples' and read their minds.

He got Murai to develop electrical caps that were supposed to synchronize the wearer's brainwaves with those of the Master by giving them shocks every few seconds in a process that was called the PSI – Perfect Salvation Initiation. Caps were given free to Asahara's inner circle, who rented or sold them at extortionate prices to the gullible. Children had to wear PSI caps, too, and were punished if they removed them.

Things began to go wrong when one of Aum's erstwhile devotees said he wanted to leave the cult. Asahara had him dunked in freezing water to remove the heat from his head that was clearly clouding his judgement. The man died from hypothermia. Another would-be deserter named Shugi Taguchi, who complained, was strangled. His body was burned and the ashes scattered. The dead man's parents contacted the police, who searched the compound but found nothing.

Then, an anti-cult lawyer named Tsutumi Sakamoto, who had already won a class-action suit against the Unification Church, took up the case of families who had lost children to Aum. Asahara gave the order to kill him. His top aides, including Murai, killed not just Sakamoto, but also his wife and their 14-month-old son.

Their bodies were put in metal drums and hidden in remote rural areas in three separate prefectures. Their teeth were smashed, so as to prevent identification from dental records. The punishment for murder in Japan was death and Asahara assured his followers that, if anyone betrayed the group, they would all die together. The killers were then ordered to burn their fingerprints off.

Soon afterwards, Asahara went to set up a branch of Aum in Germany, where he was greeted by members of the government. Taro Maki sent a *Mainichi* reporter after Asahara. At a press conference, the reporter accused Asahara of murdering Sakamoto. Asahara replied: 'If I was going to kill someone, I would kill Mr Maki.'

DIRTY TRICKS

In 1990, Asahara and 25 of his followers, all wearing Asahara masks, ran for parliament. This was not unprecedented. A secretive Buddhist sect called Soka Gakkai, suppressed in the

1930s, bounced back in the 1960s as the Komeito political party. Since the 1990s, it has been in and out of government as the junior partner in various coalitions, usually in alliance with the Liberal Democratic Party.

Aum spent £5 million ($6.5m) on the campaign and used every dirty trick in the book but got nowhere. This was a setback especially as one aide made off with £1 million ($1.3m) of Aum funds. But Asahara was not downhearted. Abandoning the Buddhist ideal of non-violence, he looked into the possibility of using weapons of mass destruction.

While Asahara and his aides made a much-publicized retreat from a comet-watching retreat on the remote island of Ishigaki, followers sprayed the Diet building in Tokyo with deadly botulism bacteria. The idea was to wipe out the government of Japan at a single stroke, but sloppy cultivation had killed the bacteria and the Japanese government survived intact.

This was another setback, but not a total disaster. The retreat had attracted thousands of new followers and Asahara netted over £1.2 million ($1.5m). Besides, Japan was small beer for Asahara. He planned to expand worldwide.

His first stop was India, but they had gurus of their own and were not impressed when Asahara announced that he was the Buddha. Similar dealings in Laos and North Korea were also unsuccessful. However, he was a hit in Russia. Broadcasting twice daily on Radio Moscow – at a cost of £500,000 ($640,000) a year – he soon had three times as many followers in Russia as he had in Japan. This was organized by his deputy Kiyohide Hayakawa, Aum's Minister of Construction, who was also involved in the murder of Shuji Taguchi and the Sakamoto family. Hayakawa's book, *Principles of a Citizen's Utopia*, was a declaration of war on the Japanese state, while Aum's Russian operation recruited military scientists, bought weapons and provided badly needed military training to loyalists.

Back in Japan, Aum started a clinic under the tender mercies of the cardiovascular surgeon, Ikuo Hayashi. He had joined the cult after a car crash, falling asleep at the wheel and putting a mother and daughter in hospital. He became depressed and turned to Aum for help. Soon, he was trying out bizarre treatments recommended by Asahara – such as swallowing hot water or string and jumping on his heart patients. The National Sanatorium Hospital had to let him go.

CLINIC OF DEATH

Hayashi ran the clinic with his wife Rira, who was an anaesthesiologist. In 18 months, nine people died in the clinic – a remarkable mortality rate considering the clinic only had nine beds.

Asahara claimed that the death rate was high because they took in a high proportion of terminal cases. Hayashi blamed it on a mysterious force. However, the place was filthy and home to numerous cockroaches, which the staff refused to kill because of the Buddhist injunction on taking life. One dead patient was left unattended on the ward for a week. On top of that, Hayashi prescribed bizarre Aum treatments, including dropping severely ill patients into baths of scalding water. He also experimented with mind control. He would implant electrodes in patients' heads and administer powerful electric shocks that often resulted in memory loss.

Families were not allowed to visit. Patients were pressurized into joining Aum and they were told that they would only be cured if they gave all their worldly goods to the cult. If that failed, patient's signatures would appear on forged wills as their condition rapidly deteriorated.

Running a hospital also gave the cult access to drugs, which were used to give initiates mystical experiences or to induce the uncertain into joining. Asahara himself was frequently tripping on LSD, which hardly aided his mental stability. Meanwhile, Asahara advanced the schedule for the Apocalypse. It would now occur in 1997. The cult's scientists were told to speed up the production of weapons of mass destruction before Japan was wiped out in a nuclear attack by the Americans.

Having failed to make a biological weapon, Aum scientists tried to make chemical ones. The nerve gas sarin was chosen as it was easy to produce and could kill vast numbers. Aum scientists started building a chemical plant to mass-produce sarin in the Mount Fuji compound.

Asahara bought a failing engineering works, bankrupted the company and looted its machine tools. These were taken to Mount Fuji where, in Aum's new factories, Hayakawa and Murai aimed to mass-produce AK-74s – the successor to the famous Kalashnikov AK-47. Laser and nuclear weapon programmes were also started. This was funded by a chain of computer shops, fast food restaurants, beauty salons, coffee shops, dating agencies, construction companies and on-line services.

These businesses brought in huge amounts of money. This was no big trick as they were staffed by Aum members who received no wages and were tax exempt because of Aum's religious status. They also acted as recruiting centres. Cut-price financing hooked the unwary. To pay off what they owed, the debtor simply had to join Aum and hand over all their worldly goods. By 1995, Aum was a billion-dollar enterprise and listed on the Tokyo stock exchange. While the cult's followers lived on practically nothing, Asahara enjoyed a luxurious lifestyle with a fleet of Rolls-Royces and Mercedes.

The Holy Monk Emperor also claimed he was above all earthly desires. But that did not stop him from having sex. He said he did not enjoy it of course, but he felt that it was his duty to initiate the young women who joined the sect. In his quarters, there was a bath that took nine at a time. He was capricious with those who took his eye. When his closest aide gave birth to twins, he replaced her with a 17-year-old who rapidly rose up the executive ladder.

Aum tried again with botulism, spraying it around at the royal wedding of the heir to the Japanese throne, Prince Naruhito, in 1993. Again, it failed, so Aum's chief microbiologist Seiichi Endo tried pumping anthrax spores out of the eighth-floor laboratory of the Aum building in eastern Tokyo. Pets grew sick and small birds died, while neighbours complained of the stench and lost their appetite. But there were no human fatalities, so Aum members were despatched to Zaire in search of the deadly Ebola virus.

With weapons production going at full tilt, security at the Aum compounds was tightened. Beatings became more frequent. Soon, people were simply disappearing. Bodies were incinerated in giant microwave ovens. The remains were then dissolved in nitric acid and flushed down the drain. And Aum hit squads went out to murder or abduct former members who were now working against them.

FULL-ON PSYCHOSIS

By the end of 1993, Aum's chief chemist, Masami Tsuchiya, began synthesizing sarin. Asahara wanted 70 tons of sarin – enough to kill millions of people – plus a stockpile of other deadly nerve gases.

Having failed to purchase a nuclear bomb in Russia, Hayakawa headed for Australia where he bought a ranch and began mining for uranium. Tsuchiya's sarin was also tested on a flock of sheep. Aum were also in trouble in Japan in a dispute over the purchase of land in Matsumoto, so Asahara decided to make a gas attack on the courthouse.

On 27 June 1994, a truck full of nerve gas turned up in Matsumoto, but the court had already risen for the day, so the truck drove over to the residential area where the judges lived and pumped out a cloud of sarin gas. However, the wind suddenly changed and the judges, although they became critically ill, did not die. Eight other people did die, though, and more than 200 were hospitalized. When one woman lapsed into an irreversible coma, His Holiness the Master Shoko Asahara sent her a package of books and invited her husband to bring her in for free treatment at the Aum hospital.

Two weeks later, there was a gas leak at the Aum facility at Kamikuishi, injuring a number of cult members. When the emergency services turned up, they found dangerous chemicals strewn all over the place, but they were quickly ejected by guards.

Aum scientists even bought supplies of materiel from the US Department of Defense. Aum purchased two remote-control helicopters as a delivery system for the sarin. But inexperienced operators crashed the £24,000 drones within minutes of delivery. They also bought a military helicopter in Chechnya and had it shipped to Japan in crates – though Aum technicians failed to reassemble it. And a nuclear bomb was still on their shopping list.

Nevertheless, Asahara decided that they were now well enough armed and started to train an army. He sent young female believers to recruit members of Japan's Self-Defence Force to train Aum volunteers in remote camps. Aum troops were told that their army would be armed with super weapons – plasma guns that vaporized anything in their path, satellites that would reflect searing beams of sunlight to fry enemies and bombs that would consume all the oxygen in the atmosphere. But if true believers had been following the meditation techniques taught by Asahara, they would survive these terrors.

PERMANENT DRUG HAZE

In preparation for his putsch, Asahara wrote a constitution for his new Supreme State and organized a shadow government – complete with a Ministry of Health and Welfare, a Ministry of Justice, a Ministry of Science and Technology and a Ministry of Construction to supervise the reconstruction of post-Apocalypse Japan. At the head of it all was the Holy Monk Emperor, Asahara himself, of course.

Meanwhile, Aum plants were producing massive amounts of drugs – LSD, mescaline, PCP or angel dust, methamphetamine and 'truth serum'. Every cult member was in a permanent drug haze and they were offloading the surplus to Japan's mafia, the *yakuza*.

One former *yakuza* boss named Kiyohide Nakada joined Aum. He bought guns from the mob and employed the expertise of mob gunsmiths at the Aum small-arms plant. Rightist *yakuza* gangs were natural allies to Aum and were also employed to kill cult members or their families for their life assurance or inheritances. They were also used for debt collection and to keep complaining neighbours quiet.

Another former *yakuza* boss, Tomomitsu Niimi, became Aum's Minister of Home Affairs, responsible for security. He maintained discipline with a rod of iron. Punishments sometimes resulted in death. Niimi's snatch squads would abduct members who had fled the cult or relatives that had money.

The National Police Agency, which was supposed to oversee local forces, had to take action when phosgene gas was pumped into the flat of Shoko Egawa, a journalist investigating Aum.

When a police informer infiltrated the Mount Fuji compound, he collapsed in the street and died. He had been given an injection of the lethal nerve gas, VX. Aum had agents in the police, so they had known he was coming. They also infiltrated other branches of the government including the judiciary and the armed forces.

Although Russian members were subdued with drugs and brainwashed in gruelling initiation rites where they were forced to eat their own vomit, they grew scared of the amount of chemicals – particularly phosgene – being stored in their headquarters and began to desert the cult. The Russian branch was damaged further when Aum's 120-strong Russian orchestra was employed to play music that Asahara said that he had heard in another dimension, which turned out to be snatches stolen from Beethoven and Tchaikovsky.

The orchestra found themselves imprisoned in the cult's Mount Fuji compound, starved and drugged. Two members escaped and managed to put a call through to the Russian embassy in Tokyo. Reluctantly, Asahara was forced to let the orchestra go.

Sarin was then being manufactured by the ton with the Aum members making it, like other Japanese factory workers, while singing a company song. In January 1995, production had to stop after sarin was found in the topsoil surrounding the Mount Fuji compound. This linked Aum with the gas attack at Matsumoto. Quickly, the chemical factory was converted into a shrine and the media were invited to inspect it. Aum claimed that sarin has been found because the government had been spraying it at them. Meanwhile, rival sects were attacked with VX nerve agent, while Aum published lists of enemies – including Emperor Akihito, President Clinton, Madonna, the Freemasons and Jews.

An earthquake hit Kobe in January 1995, killing 5,000. Asahara rushed out a book, *Disaster Nears for the Land of the Rising Sun*, saying that he had predicted it and that it had been triggered electromagnetically by the US military. Where would disaster strike next asked a flier advertising the book. On the back of the flier was a map of the Tokyo underground system.

After the brother of a member, a public notary, was abducted and killed, the Tokyo Metropolitan Police Force – the country's elite – now had to act. However, Aum planned a pre-emptive strike on the TMPF's headquarters with a laser mounted on a truck, but the equipment failed. On 5 March 1995, Aum made a practice attack on the Tokyo underground. It took place at midnight when the trains were least crowded. Nevertheless, 11 people were hospitalized.

On 15 March, another failed biological attack was made on Kasumigaseki station. As well as being home to the Japanese government, the Kasumigaseki area of Tokyo was home to both the headquarters of the Tokyo police and that National Police Agency.

By then, the TMPF had borrowed gas masks and chemical-and-biological warfare suits from the army and were planning simultaneous raids on all Aum facilities across the country on 20 March. Fearing the cult had got wind of their plans, the raids were postponed.

FULL-SCALE PANIC

Aum had its plans too. Riding the subway, they realized that they could release sarin on six trains that would arrive at Kasumigaseki station within minutes of each other, just at the time most policemen would be arriving for work.

At the Mount Fuji compound, bags of sarin solution were

prepared, while the hit squad practised piercing similar bags filled with water. Then, they each took a pill of the sarin antidote, pyridine aldoxime methiodide or PAM.

The first anyone knew of the gas attack was when a passenger pressed the emergency button at Tsukiji, four stops before Kasumigaseki. Three people collapsed on the train, five on the platform. More collapsed in the streets outside.

On the Hibiya line, there was full-scale panic at the station before Kasumigaseki. Although the victims stumbled or were carried off the carriages, the train continued and was only halted when it reached Kasumigaseki.

A leaking package on the train on the Chiyoda line was removed by two members of staff. They died. The train was evacuated at the next station.

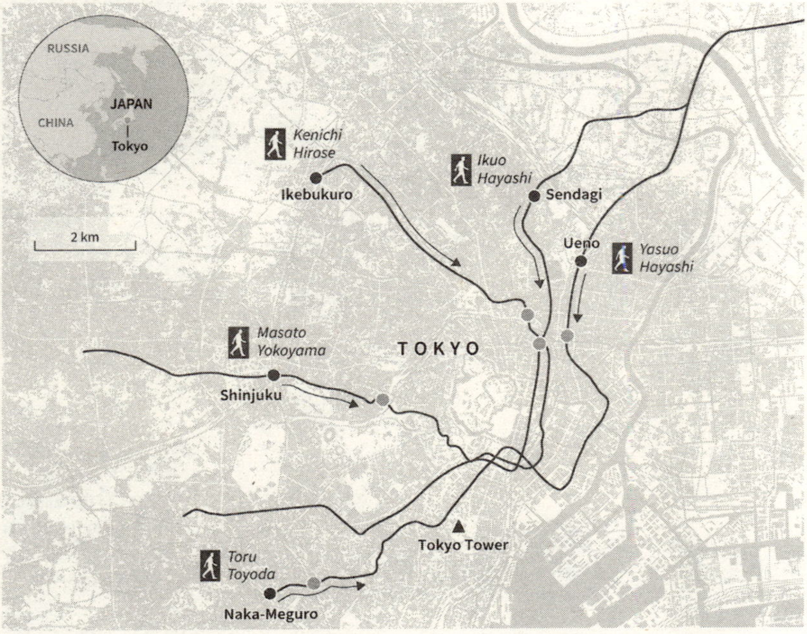

A map of the sarin gas attack in Tokyo conducted on 20 March 1995.

The train on the Marunouchi line was also allowed to continue after the first victim was helped off by staff. Another victim collapsed at the next station. The stationmaster and his assistant removed the package and the train was allowed to proceed. They fell ill and, by the time the train was stopped, one person was dead and hundreds of others affected.

A stationmaster removed the package from the train travelling in the other direction on the Marunouchi line with a dustpan and brush – but only after it had travelled through Kasumigaseki, reached the end of the line and was on its way back again. It passed through Kasumigaseki three times before the subway system was closed down at 9.30am – 80 minutes after the first victims had collapsed.

Medics were completely baffled by the symptoms of the victims coming into the emergency rooms. It was only at 10.30am that a

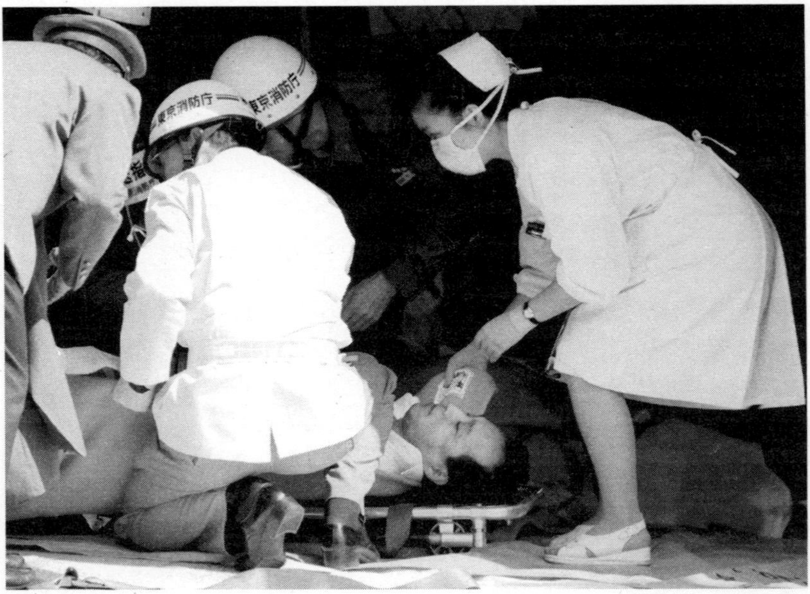

A patient is treated after the sarin gas attack on the Tokyo subway system.

military doctor recognized the symptoms of nerve gas and PAM was prescribed. By that time, some of the doctors and nurses were also developing symptoms. As the death toll mounted, it became clear that the victims were not the policemen or government officials the cultists had been targeting. They were ordinary commuters. Asahara told the killers that this was not important. The dead had the opportunity of moving on to a higher spiritual level.

MURDER VICTIMS

Aum were immediately suspected of perpetrating the attack. They were Buddhists, they said, so could have had nothing to do with the killing. At the Mount Fuji compound, stockpiles of gas and chemicals were disposed of, weapons destroyed, machinery dismantled. Asahara and his cohorts disappeared.

Two days after the gas attack, a thousand police in riot gear burst into the compound. They found people who had been incarcerated and starved. Others were too drugged to speak. Filthy and malnourished children were released, many still wearing electrode caps. In a basement, there were the ashes of numerous murder victims. The chemicals had not been concealed well and the police reckoned that Aum could have made enough sarin to kill four million people.

The cult continued to deny everything and filed a suit against the police. In a video broadcast, Asahara accused the US of trying to gas him and his followers.

Aum's offices in New York were searched and the Russian branch was closed down, with the cult being ordered to pay £2.5 million ($3.3m) in compensation to the parents of members.

Then the cult struck back. The head of the National Police Agency was shot outside his apartment building. A nationwide dragnet picked up the cult's leaders who were detained on holding charges, but Asahara remained at large. He even managed to publish a new book, *The Pity of a Ruinous Nation – Japan*, warning of another 'horrible event' soon to hit Tokyo that would 'make the Kobe earthquake seem as minor as a fly landing on your face'. It would occur on 15 April.

While the police grew increasingly frustrated, the *yakuza* changed sides. A *yakuza* hitman stabbed the cult's chief scientist, Hideo Murai, to death in front of the TV cameras outside Aum's Tokyo headquarters. Fumihiro Joyu, the former head of Aum's Russian branch, took over and Aum members insisted they had been framed by the authorities. Meanwhile, there were other gas attacks on the subway, some using hydrogen cyanide, others unrelated, and the city fell into the grip of paranoia.

All this time, Asahara was holed up in a secret hideaway in the Mount Fuji compound. On 16 May, in a blaze of publicity, the police arrested him with the TV networks on hand to broadcast the event live. The image of the purple-robed Asahara being led out of the compound was displayed on the huge TV screens that grace the sides of buildings in Tokyo.

Asahara was accused of being the mastermind behind the sarin attack. He denied it. Some of his followers saw this as an act of betrayal and revealed where caches of cyanide and sarin were hidden.

Over 350 cult members were arrested, though nearly half were released. The leadership were charged with the production of illegal drugs, kidnapping and murder. Asahara was served with ten indictments, including 27 counts of murder. Some of his disciples testified against him and in 2004 he was convicted and sentenced to death. Appeals were rejected and he was executed in 2018, along with six other cult members.

CHAPTER 8:

HEAVEN'S GATE

The founder of Heaven's Gate, Marshall H. Applewhite, called his sect 'the cult of cults'. As if to prove it, Applewhite and 38 of his followers turned themselves into angels by committing suicide in March 1997. He had convinced them that their bodies were mere containers. By destroying them, their souls would be released and beamed up to an alien spacecraft that UFO enthusiasts thought was travelling in the wake of the comet Hale-Bopp, which was visible with the naked eye from Earth at that time.

After pursuing an academic career, Applewhite quit his post at the University of St Thomas in 1970 and checked into a mental hospital in Houston, Texas. Two years later, he met a psychiatric nurse named Bonnie Lu Nettles who shared his interest in mysticism. Travelling around the US to spread their views, they gained only one convert. After six months in jail for failing to return a hire car, which he claimed he was 'divinely authorized' to keep, Applewhite set up a cult with Nettles called Human Individual Metamorphosis in California – where else?

Known as Bo and Peep, or The Two, by members of HIM, Applewhite and Nettles claimed to have been sent to Earth by aliens to teach humans how to attain a higher level of consciousness. Followers had to give up their name and their property and become celibate. They were told that they would be visited by extraterrestrials. When this did not happen, HIM fell apart.

Moving back to Texas, Applewhite took out ads inviting people to join his UFO cult, called variously Total Overcomers Anonymous and Higher Source. Those who responded were sent a video showing Applewhite and two zonked-out followers, who appeared to hang on every word that issued from the guru's lips.

UFO magazine published a feature on the cult. In it, Applewhite referred to himself as 'Do' and Nettles as 'Ti'. It is thought that these names were taken from the five-note sequence used to communicate with extraterrestrials in the 1977 movie, *Close Encounters of the Third Kind*. However, there may have been another influence. Do, aka Father John Doe or even King Do, had a special affection for *The Sound of Music*. Ti, or tea, in the 'Do-Re-Mi' song in that film was, like the poison the suicide cult took, a 'drink with jam and bread, which takes you back to Do'. Other cult members were called Re, So and Fa.

Membership again required surrendering all your property and being celibate. Applewhite and some of his senior lieutenants solved this problem by having themselves castrated.

EXPECTING TO FLY

The cult outlined its beliefs in a screenplay called *Beyond Human: Return of the Next Level*. The American TV network NBC expressed interest. Meanwhile, donations rolled in.

The cult moved into a $1.3 million (£1m) mansion set in three acres on a hilltop in San Diego County, which had once been the home of film star Douglas Fairbanks Jr. They had no contact with their wealthy neighbours. Sleeping on bunk beds, they were not allowed to drink or smoke and cut off all contact with their families. To earn money, they designed websites.

Their own website said: 'Higher Source is very much "in tune" with the current pulse and future direction of technology... The individuals at the core of our group have worked closely together for over 20 years. During those years, each of us has developed a high degree of skill and know-how through personal discipline and concerted effort. We try to stay positive in every circumstance and put the good of a project above any personal concerns or artistic egos. By sustaining this attitude and conduct, we have achieved a high level of efficiency and quality in our work. This crew-minded effort, combined with ingenuity and creativity, has helped us provide advanced solutions at highly competitive rates.'

Clearly, this attracted the San Diego Polo Club who asked Higher Source to do some more work for them early in 1997. They got an email back saying that Higher Source could not do any work after Easter, owing to a 'religious festival'.

Cult members began wearing badges saying they were 'Heaven's Gate Away Team'. Members thought of themselves as caterpillars, whose bodies were 'vehicles' or 'containers' they could leave behind when they became butterflies. The appearance of the Comet Hale-Bopp was 'the sign we've been awaiting', they said. Following unseen behind it would be 'the spacecraft to take us home'.

TASK COMPLETE

Their imminent departure was announced on the internet. 'RED ALERT – Hale-Bopp brings closure to Heaven's Gate,' their home page said. By way of explanation, Applewhite added: 'I am in the same position in today's society as was the One that was in Jesus then... If you want to go to Heaven, I can take you through that gate – it requires everything of you.' The approach of Hale-Bopp meant: 'Our 22 years of classroom here on Planet

Earth is finally coming to conclusion – "graduation" from the Human Evolutionary Level. We are happily prepared to leave "this world" and go with [the spaceship's] crew.'

The website also contains a warning: 'Planet about to be recycled – Your only chance to survive – Leave with us.'

The cult prepared for their departure by sending videos, explaining what they were going to do, to former cult members.

'By the time you get this we'll be gone – several dozen of us,' said a note accompanying the video. 'We came from the Level Above Human in distant space and we have now exited the bodies that we were wearing for our earthly task, to return to the world from whence we came – task completed.'

'We couldn't be happier about what we're about to do,' said one cult member on the video.

'Maybe they're crazy for all I know,' said a woman cultist. 'But I don't have any choice but to go for it, because I've been on this planet for 31 years and there's nothing here for me.'

Another female follower, who apparently believed – groundlessly – that Applewhite had terminal cancer, said: 'Once he is gone... there is nothing left here on the face of the Earth for me... no reason to stay a moment longer.'

FINAL PREPARATIONS

All 39 of the suicide victims appeared on the tape. They all had their hair cut short, leading the police who found the bodies to believe that they were all young men. In fact, their ages ranged from 26 to 72 and 21 of them were women.

In a second tape, Applewhite gave a long and rambling explanation of their beliefs.

'We came for the express purpose to offer a doorway to the Kingdom of Heaven at the end of this civilization, the end of the

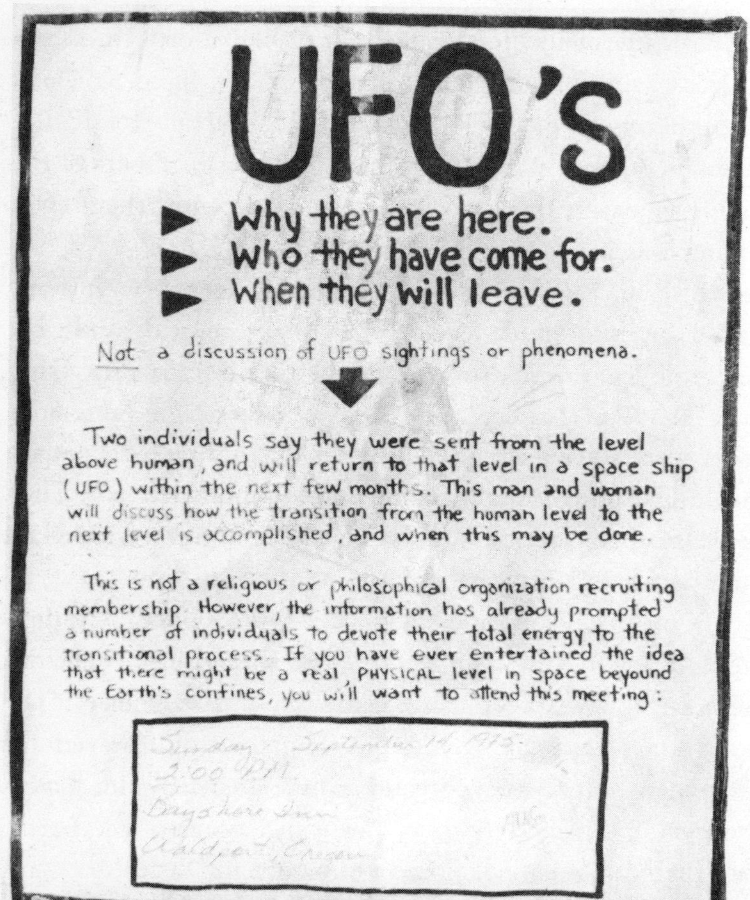

A poster for Heaven's Gate.

millennium,' he said. 'Your only chance to evacuate is to leave with us. I guess we take the prize of being the cult of cults.'

Videos despatched, the 39 members of the cult went out for a final meal in a local restaurant. They then split themselves into three groups and committed suicide in shifts over the next three days. Applewhite had thoughtfully written out suicide instructions for each member: 'Take pudding or apple sauce and mix it with the medicine' – phenobarbitone – 'drink it down with a vodka mixture and relax.'

This didn't work too well. Most of the cult members died of suffocation, perhaps inflicted on them by other members of the cult while they were drowsy. The last two suffocated themselves by pulling plastic bags over their heads.

One of the farewell videos had been sent to a Beverly Hills businessman, who employed a former member of the cult. He drove to the San Diego estate where he found 39 bodies, lying on their backs 'as if asleep'. They had their hands by their sides and they were staring at the ceiling through a three-foot square of purple silk, folded into a triangle pointing downwards. They wore identical black slacks and trainers. Their bags were packed and they carried identification details in their shirt pockets.

The Beverly Hills businessman called the police. The first two deputies who turned up were rushed to hospital. A Hazard Materials team was sent in to test for poisonous gases. The noxious fumes were discovered to have come from the victims' bodies. These were removed using a fork-lift truck and placed in a refrigerated lorry.

With their containers disposed of by the San Diego Mortuary Department, the cult members reached the spaceship which took them home – well, no one can tell them that it didn't happen.

If you want to follow suit and feel the urge to shed your container, I'm sorry but Heaven's Gate is now closed. Hale-Bopp is on its way back out into the farthest reaches of the solar system and it won't be coming back anywhere near Earth until 6210.

CHAPTER 9:

THE SOLAR TEMPLE

Heaven's Gate was not the only cult to encourage followers to take their own lives. Some 50 members of the Order of the Solar Temple died in a mass murder-suicide in October 1994.

The temple's founder, Luc Jouret, was born in what was then the Belgian Congo in 1947. After illness put paid to a career in athletics, he studied medicine at Brussels University. However, he turned away from conventional medicine and became interested in homeopathy and other forms of alternative medicine. A communist in his youth, he went to China to study traditional medicine, later travelling to India where he began to get interested in mysticism and the occult. This led him to the Golden Way Foundation, a New Age group in Geneva founded by Joseph Di Mambro, who had several convictions for fraud.

In 1981, Jouret joined the Renewed Order of the Temple, an organization that took its inspiration from the Knights Templar and led by former Gestapo officer, Julien Origas. When Origas died in 1983, the Renewed Order fell apart in a squabble over finances. Jouret left to form the International Chivalric Order of the Solar Tradition with Di Mambro. It peddled a regular mixture of environmentalism, homeopathy and mysticism. What Di Mambro added was a New Age approach to high finance.

Champagne on Ice

While the Grand Master Jouret preached that the Apocalypse was at hand, coming in the form of an ecological disaster, the 'secret master' Di Mambro made sure the fees were high and members were served chilled champagne at cult meetings. The Solar Temple were not interested in drop-outs and hippies. They wanted to recruit people with money. Jouret found new members through his upmarket homeopathic clinic in Geneva, touring the world as a corporate motivator and lecturing on environmental politics. Mugging up on the latest management techniques – along with control and coercion – Jouret realized that recruits would swallow anything as long as it was wrapped up in politically correct green packaging.

In 1986, Jouret and Di Mambro formed a Canadian chapter of the Solar Temple. They bought an old monastery in Quebec and started an organic farm. Members intent on moving there were required to sell up their property and borrow large sums of money. After all, come the Apocalypse, they wouldn't have to pay it back. Fearing that they had been duped, inmates began to accuse Jouret of financial mismanagement and the sexual exploitation of women.

But Jouret wasn't there much. He continued his corporate career, giving lectures and seminars on man-management, motivation and self-realization to large Canadian corporations. It was an opportunity to recruit corporate high-fliers. Other recruits were picked up as he travelled around giving lectures on homeopathy and wholefoods. More money came from selling inspirational tapes through New Age shops.

Membership of the Solar Temple cost $50 (£38) a week to attend lectures and seminars. For $150 (£114) a week, you got the club-class 'Club Arcadia' membership. For that, you had to work on the Temple's organic farm, recruit new members and attend the Temple's religious rites. For $200 (£150) a week, you got to join the inner 'Golden Circle', which made you privy to the Temple's secrets and occult rituals. Ultimately, though, you would also be expected to donate all your savings and your property to the Temple.

While lowly members of the cult toiled in the fields producing organic vegetables, Jouret and Di Mambro indulged in a playboy lifestyle, skiing and travelling the world. Jouret slowly tightened his grip, assuming the right to approve marriages, deciding who should have children or not and enforcing divorces. He maintained discipline by insisting that only 100 cult members – the Elect – would survive the Apocalypse. Of course, it was Jouret who was to decide who these people would be.

DEATH OF A PRINCESS

One of the cult's most prestigious converts was Princess Grace of Monaco, the former film star Grace Kelly, who was recruited shortly before her death in 1982. According to an article that appeared in the *Sunday Times*, her initiation into the cult involved nude massage and ritual sex. A former security guard at the cult said that Di Mambro asked her to donate 20 million Swiss francs ($23m/£17.5m) to the temple. She agreed to pay 12 million francs ($14m/£10m) into a bank in Zurich but then began to have doubts and quarrelled with Di Mambro. Shortly afterwards, she was out driving with her younger daughter, Stephanie, when their car crashed down a mountainside, landing, bizarrely, in a garden of another Solar Temple member. Kelly was pulled alive from the wreckage but had suffered serious injuries and died in hospital the next day.

Details of what was going on in the cult began to come out when a cult member left in disgust and went to the newspapers after claiming they had handed over $500,000 (£390,000) to the sect. Then, in 1993, Jouret was fined $1,000 (£780) on weapons charges. By that time, there was growing disquiet in the Canadian branch of the Temple. During the 1980s, Di Mambro had invested the Temple's funds heavily in property, but now the market was in decline. The yuppie dream was over and so was its New Age religion. Soon, Jouret began to talk of 'transit'. Apparently, a fiery death was required.

The chosen few would leave their bodies and undergo a spiritual journey to the star Sirius, though Venus and Jupiter were mooted as other destinations. None of these places, on

Grace Kelly, Princess of Monaco and member of the Order of the Solar Temple.

the face of it, seem very appealing to live in, but some believers, apparently, were eager to go.

ENDGAME

On the night of 5 October 1994, a farmhouse in the farming village of Cheiry in Switzerland caught fire. The owner, retired businessman Albert Giacobino, was found dead in the bedroom. He had been shot. In the grounds a spacious barn had been converted into a temple of sorts. Over a triangular pulpit was a picture of Christ holding a chalice, though the face was that of Jouret. A pentagram had been painted on the floor. On it, spread out in a sunburst, were 23 dead bodies – 12 women, ten men and Di Mambro's 12-year-old daughter. The women were wearing robes of white and gold; the men white, black and red.

The cult members seemed to have been well prepared for their journey. Empty champagne bottles were strewn around. But they may all have been willing travellers. They had been drugged with sleeping pills. Some had plastic bags tied over their faces. Others had been shot up to eight times.

Four hours later, three chalets in Granges-sur-Salvan, 50 miles (80 km) away, caught fire. Inside, there were 25 bodies, five of them belonging to children. They had been injected with poison. Later that day, there was a fire at a house owned by the Solar Temple in Quebec. The bodies of a man and a woman were found in the bedroom. Around their necks, they had medallions with a double-headed eagle, indicating they were members of the Solar Temple. Firefighters found the bodies of Antonio Dutoit, Di Mambro's Swiss chauffeur, and his British wife, Nicki, in the basement. They had been killed in ritualistic fashion. Wedged behind the immersion heater was their three-month-old son, Christopher. He had a plastic bag over his head and a stake through his heart.

Former cult members claimed that Di Mambro had been angry that the Dutoits had had a baby without permission. The child, Di Mambro said, was the anti-Christ and ordered cult members to kill it. Jouret and Di Mambro were seen leaving the house the day before the fire. They took the 10am flight to Geneva and had then gone about finishing off the rest of the cult in Switzerland.

At first, it was thought that Jouret and Di Mambro were involved in some financial swindle and had escaped with the proceeds. However, dental records showed that Jouret and Di Mambro were among the victims of the fire in Granges-sur-Salvan.

In December 1995, 14 more members of the Solar Temple, including three children, were found dead near Grenoble in a circular star-formation in an isolated clearing on the Vercors massif, near Saint-Pierre-de-Chérennes in France. They had been sedated with pills, then shot in the head, doused with gasoline and set on fire. Two other bodies were found nearby, apparently of the perpetrators. They, too, were shot in the head.

And on 22 March 1997, the charred bodies of three women and two men were found in a house owned by a member of the Solar Temple in Saint Casimir, Quebec. Three teenage children were found drugged nearby. They were to have died with the others, but had persuaded their parents to let them live. However, as the drugs took hold, the adults found it difficult to set the house on fire, so the children did it for them.

CHAPTER 10:

THE PEOPLES TEMPLE

When it comes to murder-suicide, it is hard to beat cult leader Jim Jones, founder of the Peoples Temple. He was responsible for the death of over 900 of his followers. There was, perhaps, a more sinister side to his interest in moggies.

Born in 1931, Jones was brought up in the small town of Lynn in Indiana. His family were dirt poor and lived in a shack without electricity or running water. Jones' father had been gassed in France during World War I and was in and out of hospital. His mother was forced to go out to work, so he was neglected, sometimes walking around naked until the women of the town took pity on him.

A precocious child, he began his career in religion at the age of 12, delivering hellfire-and-damnation speeches at mock funerals for dead cats, which neighbours said he had killed himself, possibly as sacrifices. His mother believed in spells, omens, black magic and the transmigration of souls.

She also made up bedtime stories for her son, which featured imaginary journeys up the Amazon and her life with the head-hunters there. She believed that dreams were visions of the future and predicted her son would one day be the champion of the poor and the weak. He was destined to be a man who left his mark on the world, she said.

SEARCH FOR BELIEF

As World War II started, he became an admirer of Adolf Hitler, giving the Nazi salute to German prisoners of war who were on their way to a POW camp. A voracious reader, he also studied Joseph Stalin, Karl Marx and Mahatma Gandhi. Later, Mao Zedong became his hero.

Of his childhood, Jones said: 'I was ready to kill by the end of the third grade. I mean, I was so aggressive and hostile, I was ready to kill. Nobody gave me love, any understanding. In those days, a parent was supposed to go with a child to school functions. There was some kind of school performance, and everybody's parent was there but mine. I'm standing there, alone. Always was alone.'

While his father was a dyed-in-the-wool racist and a lifelong member of the Ku Klux Klan, Jones abhorred the discrimination against African-Americans he saw all around him. For years, he would not speak to his father after he refused to allow Jones to bring one of his black friends home.

ON HIS OWN PATH

When his contemporaries left school to make their way in the white world of banking, business, farming or teaching, Jones worked in a hospital in Richmond, Indiana, where his colleagues were mainly poor and black. There, he met and married a student nurse, five years his senior, named Marceline Mae Baldwin. He would abuse her psychologically by telling her that close friends or family members were dead, only telling her later that it was untrue.

Jones enrolled at the University of Indiana in Bloomington to study medicine. After a year, he dropped out, now intent on becoming a preacher, even though he told his wife that he was an atheist. The best way to demonstrate his growing belief in Marxism, he decided, was to infiltrate the church.

In 1952, he became a student pastor in the Methodist church and began a project to open a playground for children of all races. Soon, he was dismissed, ostensibly for stealing church funds, though he claimed that it was because he had tried to integrate the congregation.

He joined the Second Wave of Pentecostalism under self-proclaimed prophet, William Branham, and started his own Community Unity Church. Buying a building in a racially mixed section of Indianapolis, Jones renamed his church the Wings of Deliverance, then the Peoples Temple Full Gospel Church, later the Peoples Temple Christian Church Full Gospel and finally just the Peoples Temple. Jones' purported clairvoyant revelations attracted spiritualists.

In 1956, he was ordained in the Independent Assemblies of God, part of the Latter Rain movement. One of its key tenets was the Manifested Sons of God, which promised believers supernatural gifts and superhuman abilities heralding the second coming of Christ.

Jones was not the prototype American tele-evangelist, preaching God, the Flag and the American way. Quite the opposite. In 1953, he had joined the Communist Party. That year, he had conceived of the idea of 'revolutionary death' when atom spies Julius and Ethel Rosenberg were executed. Their deaths, he thought, had shattered the illusion that America was the 'last best hope of mankind'. Jones described himself privately as a 'socialist', though his political philosophy seems to owe more to Robin Hood than to Karl Marx. The poorer and weaker his followers, the more attention he lavished on them. One early member of the church recalled: 'He had a lot of them, the kind of people most folks don't want to have anything to do with. Fat, ugly old ladies who didn't have nobody in the world.

He'd pass around hugs and kisses like he really loved them, and you could see on their faces what he meant to them.'

His success at building a truly multi-racial congregation – one of the first in America – attracted unwelcome attention. A swastika was placed on the Temple, a stick of dynamite was left in a Temple coal pile, and a dead cat was thrown at Jones' house after a threatening phone call. Undaunted, he adopted eight Korean and black children. His unwavering stand against racism led, in 1960, to his appointment as director of the newly created City Human Rights Commission, reporting directly to the mayor.

Reverend Jim Jones.

THE KEY TO SUCCESS

Jones had made several pilgrimages to the Peace Mission of Father Divine in Philadelphia, which was the most successful ministry to the urban poor in the country. He learned that key to Father Divine's success was his insistence on his own divinity and extravagant demonstrations of the power of faith. Jones quickly learned the lesson and began putting on his own displays of healing. In carefully contrived theatrical settings, he got believers to spew up chicken livers, claiming they were cancers. He raised up perfectly fit young people made up to look like wheelchair-bound geriatrics who found that they suddenly, and on cue, could stand.

He also astounded his congregation with his mind-reading powers. This was a trick, too. He had trusted followers interview potential recruits to ask them detailed question on the pretext of an unrelated examination. This provided Jones with inside information that would make him seem clairvoyant and in possession of superhuman powers.

Jones also noted that Father Divine, though black with an almost exclusively African-American following, surrounded himself with an inner circle of attractive, middle-class white women. Father Divine also compensated himself for the long hours of selfless devotion to his flock with Cadillacs and a 40-room mansion. At the age of 70, he married a 21-year-old Canadian but insisted that the marriage was chaste. His young wife thwarted Jones' attempt to take over the mission, claiming to be the reincarnation of Divine after he died.

Fearing nuclear war, he sought safety in South America. He took his young family off for two years' missionary work in the *favelas* of Brazil. There, he kept quiet about being a Marxist and maintained that he was promoting a form of anti-capitalism he called 'Apostolic socialism'. On his way, Jones stopped off to preach in British Guiana, which was soon to become the independent country of Guyana.

THE PROMISED LAND

Back in the US, the Peoples Temple was falling apart with financial troubles and dwindling attendance. Jones decided that he must take his followers to a 'promised land'. Redwood Valley near Ukiah in California was the place where he relocated the Peoples Temple, bussing his followers across the country to their new home. Some stayed behind in Indiana, but those who followed sold all their property and gave it to the church. From Redwood Valley, the Temple spread into San Francisco and Los Angeles. Followers were bussed across the state to run food kitchens and day-care centres. Soon, he was wielding considerable political power.

Jones could deliver the several thousand members of his Temple as a block vote. Virtually every liberal officeholder in the state – from lieutenant governor down to district attorney – was offered the chance to address his congregation. They quickly became beholden to Jones. In gratitude for the Temple's support, San Francisco's mayor, George Moscone, appointed Jones chairman of the city's Housing Authority. For his part, Jones used his influence to secure preferential treatment of his congregation at welfare agencies, housing authorities and in court.

Even national politicians cultivated him. During the 1976 presidential campaign, Jones was invited to dine with Rosalynn Carter, presidential hopeful Jimmy Carter's wife. Behind the scenes, Jones began taking illicit drugs. His growing paranoia was further fuelled by accusations that he demanded sexual favours from women in the congregation and raped several men, but he kept his flock in line by prophesying that fires, car accidents and death or injury would come upon anyone unfaithful to him and his teachings.

In affluent Redwood Valley, the Peoples Temple attracted an educated white middle-class congregation, which he installed as an upper echelon called the Planning Commission to organize the Temple's communal lifestyle. An ambitious young lawyer named Tim Stoen was one of his lieutenants. Like many of his generation Stoen had been disillusioned by the assassination of John F. Kennedy, the Vietnam war and the race riots that were tearing the country apart. He was looking for a revolutionary way ahead. Jones' multi-racial congregation and free-wheeling

Tim and Grace Stoen.

Christian/Marxist philosophy seemed to represent the wave of the future. Jones' political influence secured Stoen the plum job of Assistant District Attorney in San Francisco. The price tag was sex with Stoen's attractive young wife, Grace.

In January 1972, Grace gave birth to a son, John-John. The birth certificate listed the father as Tim Stoen. But in an affidavit, Stoen stated that he requested Jones to sire a child by his wife 'in the steadfast hope that the said child will become the devoted follower of Jesus Christ and be instrumental in bringing God's kingdom here on Earth, as has been his wonderful natural father'. Jim Jones, Tim Stoen said, was the 'most compassionate, honest and courageous human being on Earth'. The affidavit was witnessed by Marceline, Jones' wife. Grace Stoen's opinion was not recorded, but she left the church in 1976, leaving the child behind.

SEX AND POWER

Jones used sex, not just for pleasure, but for power. By seducing members of his congregation, he loosened the bond between them and their sexual partner, binding them both closer to the Temple. Jones banned all sexual contact with outsiders and sexual relations between members of the congregation required the Temple's specific approval, in advance. It was seldom forthcoming. One woman had an abortion, rather than bear Jones' child, but at least three of Jones' congregation carried his children to term.

Jones did not just sleep with the women. Male congregation members were also encouraged to have sex with him. This, Jones explained, was a 'revolutionary act'. He forced every member of the Peoples Temple to say they were homosexual, while proclaiming himself the only heterosexual, though this was clearly untrue. Women who slept with him claimed he was the best lover they ever had. Peoples Temple member, Tim Carter, felt Jones 'put them up to that kind of talk'.

But Jones entered into the spirit of things with a little too much zest. In 1973, he was picked up for making flagrant homosexual overtures to an undercover LAPD vice officer, allegedly masturbating in front of him in the toilet of a cinema during a matinee screening of *Jesus Christ Superstar*. Jones had enough influence not only to get the charges dropped, but also to have records of the arrest sealed by a Los Angeles judge.

Sex was a frequent topic of discussion at the Temple's all-important Planning Commission, with Jones railing against bourgeois sexual attitudes. Members would be forced to confess their sexual fantasies and fears. Those less than forthcoming would be condemned to long periods of celibacy. At one meeting, Jones forced one white man to perform cunnilingus on a black woman to prove that he harboured no racial prejudice. Sexual candour and public urination, Jones maintained, were symbolic representations of the Temple's openness. Jones, it seemed to some, took an unhealthy pleasure in exhibiting himself.

PARANOID DELUSIONS

Meanwhile, Jones began to take on a more paranoid view of the outside world. He claimed that his phone was being tapped and that he was being followed by government agents. People who had left the Peoples Temple were watched by members to make sure they were not talking to the FBI or hostile journalists. Blackmail was also employed to ensure their silence. The Mertle family were typical victims.

In 1968, Elmer and Deanna Mertle visited the Peoples Temple in Redwood Valley. They found there a warmth and sense of community that they had not experienced before. It was like a family, with Jones styling himself 'Dad'.

Deanna was brought up a Seventh Day Adventist and Jones

challenged many of her fundamental beliefs. Christianity was a 'slave religion' and the Bible was full of logical contradictions, he said. She read it again and found that it was.

Elmer was more attracted by Jones' left-wing politics. And he liked the way, after their first visit to the Temple, everyone greeted them by name. From the off, the Mertles and their children were fussed over like they already belonged. Soon, they had sold their home and given all their money to the Temple, moving into a farm that Jones had rented for them nearby. By 1975, the Mertles were members of the Planning Commission, but they became increasingly disturbed by Jones' bizarre behaviour. And when their 16-year-old daughter was spanked for a minor infraction, they decided to leave.

This would not be so easy. Everything they had belonged to the Temple, which was also their only source of income. They had been completely supported by it for five years and had had almost no contact with the outside world. They were lucky, though. Elmer's mother was rich and she bailed them out.

When Deanna Mertle told the Temple they were leaving, they were accused of stealing incriminating documents from the church. Jones threatened to smear Elmer as a paedophile. The Mertles fled and changed their names, depositing sworn affidavits charging Jones with all manner of indecent behaviour in a safe-deposit box to ensure their safety. Jones responded by denouncing them as traitors, who had sold out their brothers and sisters in the Temple 'for a pocketful of credit cards and a fancy car'.

'HUMANITARIAN OF THE YEAR'

That same year, the Foundation for Religion in America picked Jones as one of their '100 Outstanding Clergymen in America' and Jones was named 'Humanitarian of the Year' by the *Los Angeles*

Herald-Examiner. On Memorial Day 1977, Jim Jones was invited to speak at an anti-suicide rally in San Francisco to persuade the city fathers to build a barrier along the Golden Gate Bridge – a favourite jumping-off point for the depressed and disturbed. Although Jones' speech began on a stern moral condemnation of suicide, halfway through it became a blanket endorsement of it.

Jones had first mentioned the idea of 'revolutionary suicide' to Grace Stoen in 1973. While he planned for his followers to die, he said he would stay alive to explain why they had done it. In 1976, he began to put his plan into practice. After railing against the 'traitors' who had left the Temple, he told the congregation that they had to prove their loyalty by drinking a cordial laced with poison he had prepared. Forty-five minutes later, when none of them had died, he told them that there was no poison in the drink. He had only been testing them.

This was the first of a series of suicide rehearsals that Jones called 'white nights'. Each time the congregation were told that they were swallowing poison – and they could never be sure they were not. But gradually they got used to the idea of laying down their life for 'Dad' – who by now was claiming to be God, or at the very least a being from another planet like Superman.

Then, in March 1977, *New West* magazine published an article attacking the Temple. The Mertles had told a reporter about the sexual and physical abuse they had witnessed. The article also outlined Grace Stoen's relationship with Jones. She now began suing the Temple for custody of her son. Jones was determined that she should not have him. John-John was one of the new breed of followers born into the Temple, who Jones was determined would inherit the Earth.

As Jones' legal advisor, Tim Stoen told him that there was no point in fighting Grace in the American courts. They were bound to return John-John to his natural mother – especially if the Mertles gave evidence about Jones' bizarre sexual practices. There was only one way that Jones could hold on to John-John. That was to take him abroad. Fighting for custody in a foreign court could be strung out for years, perhaps for ever.

SOCIALIST UTOPIA

Since his first fleeting visit to Guyana in 1963, Jones had come up with plans to build a socialist Utopia there. The left-wing Guyanese government were immediately receptive. In 1974, Jones paid $1 million (£775,000) for 27,000 acres of jungle in Guyana, where he established an experimental agricultural outpost, which was soon known as 'Jonestown'. Then, in 1977, when Jones came under increasing pressure in the US, large amounts of building

A group of Jonestown residents and new arrivals, 1978.

material were shipped up the river to nearby Port Kaituma. Some 380 cult members applied for visas and headed for Guyana. John-John was among them. The following year, another 700 set off.

On the way, they enjoyed a brief period of freedom; inside the compound at Jonestown, iron discipline was re-imposed. Casual sexual encounters were banned. This did not apply to Jones himself, of course. Moving into a hut with two of his mistresses, and with his wife living nearby, he had his pick of the flock. One young girl who refused his advances was drugged and taken to Jones' hut each night. But a young woman named Debbie Blakely was expelled. Jones said she had wanted bourgeois sex – for pleasure! For him, sex was a political act.

Those who found favour with Jones were awarded special privileges. The Jonestown doctor, who supported Jones' claim that 'non-revolutionary sex' caused cancer, was indulged with a succession of teenage girls. Those who opposed him suffered. Beatings were commonplace for minor offences or simply because Jones thought that the offender's 'head was between their legs' – that is, they were thinking about sex rather than socialist work. This especially applied to any male who showed an interest in a girl he fancied.

Adults were forced to fight each other until 'right prevailed' or simply they were beaten into bloody submission. Children were especially harshly treated. They were caned before a microphone, so that their cries echoed from the PA throughout the compound. Others were lowered down a well.

While cult members toiled in the fields from sun-up to sundown on meagre rations, Jones stayed in his hut taking drugs, gorging himself and monitoring the news from San Francisco and the Temple's office in Guyana's capital, Georgetown. He claimed that Jonestown was about to be attacked by a force of mercenaries trained by the CIA. Armed guards were posted around the compound, ostensibly to protect the compound from attack but actually they were there to stop disaffected cult members from escaping.

THE INVESTIGATORS ARRIVE

Back in the US, a support group called the Committee of Concerned Relatives was formed. One of these relatives was Sam Houston, a journalist with the Associated Press, who accused the cult of murdering his son. The boy had left the Temple after a row with Jones. The next day, he had died in a railroad accident. Houston was a friend of Congressman Leo Ryan. Several of the Temple's members came from Ryan's congressional district.

On 24 October 1978, Ryan received authorization from the US House of Representatives' Foreign Affairs Committee to go to Guyana to investigate the Temple's settlement there. With legal action threatening to cut off the cult's funds, Jones had no choice but to permit the visit. However, he tried to stipulate that Ryan could not bring any 'traitors' or the press with him. But the congressman would have none of it. He turned up in Guyana with four members of the Committee of Concerned Relatives, reporters and photographers, plus an NBC film crew.

On the afternoon of 17 November, Ryan's party flew to the airstrip at Port Kaituma, a few miles from Jonestown. They were picked up by one of Jones' adopted sons, Johnny. Congressman Ryan, the relatives and the party of journalists entered Jonestown just before sunset. The reception was surprisingly friendly. Although Jones retired to his hut, cult members had been told to smile. After dinner was served at eight, the Jonestown band began to play. Congressman Ryan made a speech.

'From what I have seen,' he said, 'there are a lot of people who believe this is the best thing that ever happened to them.'

Even the cult members broke into spontaneous applause. The tension was dispelled. The band struck up again. But things were not as they seemed. Temple member, Vernon Gosney, passed a note to NBC reporter, Don Harris, asking him to help him and his friend, Monica Bagby, to leave Jonestown with Congressman Ryan the next day.

JONES BEGINS TO CRACK

At dawn the following day, nine sect members seized their chance to escape. They set off through the jungle towards the village of Matthew's Ridge, some 20 miles (32 km) away. While Ryan was given a guided tour of Jonestown, some journalists began poking around on their own as Don Harris began interviewing Jones on camera. Jones talked openly about his mistresses and denied press reports that there was a ban on sexual intercourse among his followers, saying that 30 babies have been born there since the summer of 1977.

But this was not the smooth polyester-suited Jim Jones who had charmed politicians in California. Jones was now fat, pale and sweaty. After only a few minutes of persistent questioning, Jones began to crack.

'The only thing I regret is that somebody hasn't shot me,' he ranted. 'We're only a small community, we're no threat to anyone, but they won't rest until they destroy us. I wish they would just shoot me and get it over with. But I guess the media smear is what they use now – in the long run it is as good as assassination.'

Other reporters asked Jones about John-John, who Jones still refused to return to his mother. By this time, Tim Stoen had also defected from the Peoples Temple and was reconciled with his wife. But as Stoen had predicted, the custody case was stalled in the Guyanese courts.

Reporters asked why the Jonestown security guards carried weapons and why threats were made to those who wanted to leave.

'It's all lies,' responded Jones wearily. But then one of his henchmen brought news that Edith Parks, the grandmother of a family that had been planning to escape for some time, had asked Congressman Ryan to take them out.

'I am betrayed,' wailed Jones. 'It never stops.'

Following Parks' lead, another 20 people asked Ryan to take them with him. Jones, by this time, was apoplectic.

'I've given my life for my people,' he cried.

But Jones was persuaded to let them go. What was the 30 who wanted to leave, his aides said, compared with the thousand who wanted to stay? But then, a husky young man in his late-20s, named Don Sly, pulled a knife from his pocket and tried to stab Congressman Ryan. Two of Jones' aides grabbed Sly and pulled him away.

ALL HELL BREAKS LOOSE

At the last moment, one of the Temple's security guards named Larry Layton announced that he was 'pissed off with Jonestown' and wanted to leave. He joined Ryan and his departing entourage.

Two planes waited at the airstrip in Port Kaituna. Layton got on. Somehow, he had managed to smuggle a gun on board. Before the plane could take off, the Jonestown tractor turned up, pulling a trailer carrying 20 armed men. On board the plane, Layton started shooting, hitting Monica Bagby in the chest. Then, men from the trailer opened up, killing Congressman Ryan, Temple member Patricia Parks, photographer Greg Robinson, Don Harris and an NBC cameraman, who managed to shoot a few seconds of film before he died. Others manage to flee into the jungle.

When Jones heard that some had escaped, he knew the game was up. When the news got back to the United States, the CIA would force the left-wing government in Georgetown to send soldiers of the Guyanese Defence Force to seize Jonestown. He called his followers together at the main pavilion.

THE BAD NEWS

Sitting on a crude wooden throne, surrounded by nearly a thousand of his followers, he gave them the bad news. They were about to die. Guyanese soldiers coming to get them were their black socialist brothers, so they could not fight back. It was too late to escape to the Soviet Union, though he had already despatched three of his aides to the Soviet embassy in Georgetown with a suitcase that contained half-a-million dollars in cash (£380,000). But the Russians would not take them now. It would be an embarrassment. The only answer was the 'revolutionary suicide' they had long prepared for.

Jonestown's medical staff prepared two 50-gallon drums of grape Flavor-Aid, laced with a cocktail of cyanide, valium and various other sedatives and tranquillizers. Jones told his congregation that they should not be afraid to die. They were simply 'stepping over to another plane and they would meet again in another place'.

Most of the cult members took him at his word and queued up in orderly fashion. Jones ordered that the children should die first. Mothers gave the deadly drink to their offspring. Infants had it squirted in their mouths from a needle-less syringe. Even Jones' own children meekly took the poison.

Jones had long said that swallowing poison would lead to a

painless death. But when the children went into convulsions, panic broke out. Jones assured his congregation: 'They are not crying out of pain. It's just a little bitter tasting.'

Then Jones asked a question: 'Can some people assure these children of the relaxation of stepping over into the next plane?'

He calmed the hysterics, saying: 'This is not the way for people who are socialists or communists to die. No way for us to die. We must die with some dignity.'

As they were surrounded by armed guards, they had a simple choice: either drink the poison or die at the hands of Jones' henchmen. Resigned to their fate, the adults calmly took their poison from paper cups. Then they went out into the fields and lay down and died. Then came the turn of the armed guards. They, too, took their poison without resistance.

The whole event was recorded on a 45-minute audio tape. On it, Jones can be heard reassuring his followers. 'I don't care how many screams you hear... how many anguished cries; death is a million times preferable... Take the potion like they used to take it in ancient Greece. It is a revolutionary act.'

At the end of tape, he left a message for the world. 'We didn't commit suicide,' he said. 'We committed an act of revolutionary suicide protesting the conditions of an inhumane world.'

Then came a note of self-pity. 'The world is not ready for me,' he lamented.

Finally, Jones took a pistol and blew his brains out. Annie Moore, one of Jonestown's nurses, shot herself in the head with the same gun moments later.

That was not the end of it. Jones had already radioed the Temple's office in Georgetown, explained the situation and instructed them to commit suicide too. When the police arrived, Sharon Amos, the Temple's public relations officer, took her three small children into the bathroom, killed them, then slit her own throat. The three aides who had taken the money to the Soviet embassy did not follow suit, though one of them committed suicide four months later at a press conference after reading a statement explaining what had happened at Jonestown and blaming the US government.

FINAL DEATH TOLL

As Jones predicted, the Guyanese army was sent to Jonestown. It was only when a US army mortuary team arrived in Jonestown that the death toll was finally fixed at 909; 276 of those people were children. Among the dead was Grace Stoen's son, John-John.

With the exception of a few feeble old people, there were no signs of telltale blisters on the upper arms that would indicate that the cyanide had been forcibly injected into unwilling victims. Although they had been ringed by armed guards, they did not seem to need to coerce the cult members into killing themselves. In fact, the victims seemed not just willing but eager to drink the poison. According to one survivor, the first victim, Ruletta Paul, walked up to the dais with her child and took the cyanide without even being asked.

'She just poured it down the baby's throat. And then she took the rest herself,' said the witness. 'It didn't take them right away. She had time to walk outside... then the next woman, Michelle Wilson, she came up with her baby and did the same thing.'

Although one could argue that the suicides were voluntary, the coroner's court found that Jones 'and persons unknown' were responsible for the deaths at Jonestown. Jones had spent years cowing his followers into total submission. Not only would they do whatever he said, they would anticipate what he wanted and do it before he even asked. Had he lived, Jim Jones would certainly have been charged with murder.

SURVIVORS

Not everyone had perished. The day after the massacre, Guyanese soldiers entering Jonestown found two survivors. Grover Davis was hard of hearing and missed the announcement calling everyone to gather at the pavilion. When he finally went to find out what was going on, he saw the first child victims in their death throes. He hid in a dry well. The next day, he climbed out and went back to his hut to sleep. He woke when the soldiers arrived and was nearly shot. They thought that he was a corpse coming back to life again.

Frail and bedridden, Hyacinth Thrush had slept through the whole thing. When her breakfast did not turn up the next morning, she hobbled outside to find out what was happening. The terrible smell of bodies rotting in the tropical sunshine explained everything. Later, she said she was sorry to have missed the opportunity to die with her brothers and sisters.

Former soldier Odell Rhodes also escaped. He had been a heroin addict when he first encountered the Peoples Temple. It had turned his life around. After being weaned off drugs, he became a teacher and he was happy to go to Guyana. But, later,

Bodies in Jonestown after the mass suicide.

he spoke of it as a prison. The inmates were held there by fear of the Temple, fear of Jim Jones, fear of the security squad and fear that unspecified forces in the United States would destroy them if they got free.

Rhodes said he had once written a letter to Jones asking to leave and was given extra work assignments as a punishment. Another man, he said, was beaten for having the same temerity.

What he particularly disliked were the nightly meetings. After a long day in the fields, he could not stand the hysteria, the sermonizing, the sexual humiliation and the white nights, so he volunteered to work in the nursing cottage, which meant he could skip the meetings. Missing out on the nightly indoctrination, he was not prepared to take the poison on Jones' say-so.

At the final meeting, Rhodes found himself at the front – unable to get away without drawing attention to himself. He was shocked at how willingly the others took the poison. When the children started dying, he volunteered to go to the hospital to get a stethoscope. After hiding under a house, he slipped out into the jungle. When he reached Port Kaituma 6 miles (10 km) away, he found it difficult to convince the local police that everyone at Jonestown was dead. Eventually, they put him on the phone to Georgetown, where a sceptical police inspector said that he would go there the next morning with the army.

Another escapee was Stanley Clayton. He was working in the kitchen that evening when the call to assemble came.

'A security guard came into the kitchen, pointed a pistol at everybody and told us all to go to the pavilion,' he said. Jones had already ordered preparations for a mass suicide to be started. But one woman, Christine Miller, was protesting. 'She was telling Jones she had a right to do what she wanted with her own life. Guards with guns and bows and arrows pressed in on her, and Jones tried to make her understand that she had to do it.'

Then a truck drove up to the pavilion.

'The people in the truck rushed up to Jones. He announced that Congressman Ryan was dead and we had to do what we had to do. He told the nurses to hurry with the potion. He told them to take care of the babies. He said any survivors would be castrated and tortured by the Guyanese army. The nurses started taking the babies from the mothers. Jones kept saying: "Hurry, hurry!" But the people were not responding. The guards then moved in and started pulling people, trying to get them to take the potion.'

Security guards were pulling people up from their seats telling them that they must go. Meanwhile Jones was beseeching and cajoling them. Clayton recalled: 'He kept telling them: "I love you. I love you. It is nothing but a deep sleep. It won't hurt you. It's just like closing your eyes and drifting into a deep sleep."'

He gave the inquest a vivid account of mothers and nurses lifting cups of cyanide-laced drinks to the lips of babies and of some women injecting the poison into their children.

'There were mothers and people crying,' he said, 'and Jim came across on the speakers telling them to "Shut up. Don't be scaring the babies like that. Make them feel happy." He was saying they have to die proud with dignity.'

Clayton said that it seemed that many thought they were participating in one of the 'white night' drills and that they were not actually taking poison.

'After mostly the babies were gone, I would say, people began realizing this was really taking place,' he testified.

It was at this point, he said, that many men and women seemed reluctant to continue the death ceremony and Jones stepped into the crowd and began guiding them toward the poison vat. Jones' wife, Marceline, also walked among the followers, hugging them and saying: 'I'll see you in your next life.'

Clayton said he had seen enough. By then, he reckoned all but 100 to 200 people had died.

'It was dark by now. I went around to each of the guards, embraced them and told them: "I'll see you later." I skipped out into the bushes. All the time I kept saying to myself: "I can't believe this. Jim Jones is mad."'

Some 30 to 45 minutes later, Clayton said he heard what sounded like a chorus of cheers from Jonestown.

'What I heard, I would say was three cheers,' he told the coroner's court. 'It sounded like a lot of people. It was just a lot of voices.'

When he tried to re-enter Jonestown to recover his passport, he heard five gunshots and dropped back into the jungle. He went back, but as he pulled his passport out from an office file, he heard another shot. He switched off the light and waited several minutes before slipping out along the main dirt road. He found a house nearby and told the occupants what had happened. They did not believe him. But, when he told them that they would be able to help themselves to the tools and supplies in Jonestown, they decided to check out what he was saying. They came back with their arms full of stolen goods and a glazed look of horror in their eyes.

AFTERMATH

When Clayton finally made it into town, he was arrested. News of the massacre had got out and it was rumoured that one of Jones' last acts was to send out assassination squads. It was thought that Clayton belonged to one of them. He eventually managed to convince the police otherwise.

Others survived because they were away from Jonestown at the time. Three of Jones' sons were with the Peoples Temple's basketball team playing in Georgetown that night. One of them was 19-year-old Stephan, who said he could not forgive his father for what happened.

'I can almost say I hate the man. He has destroyed everything I have to live for,' he said. His father 'claimed he was afraid of nothing, which I know was bull. My father was a very frightened man.'

There was one final terrible irony in Jim Jones' death. While he had dedicated his ministry to helping black people and saw himself as a great revolutionary leader in the mould of Martin Luther King and Malcolm X, the cyanide turned the skin of even the white cult members black, but Jones, who had shot himself, had been drained of blood and turned a deathly white.

Even with Jones dead, his former followers were not safe. After the Jonestown Massacre, the Mertles and their teenage daughter were found murdered. No one has ever been caught for the crime and the police have no suspects and no active leads. Although the police said they had no reason to believe that their murders had anything to do with the Peoples Temple, others who had left the cult disagreed. Many lived for years in fear of the Temple's assassination squads.

Only one person went on trial for complicity in the Jonestown Massacre. It was 35-year-old, ex-Quaker, Larry Layton. Extradited to the United States, he was charged with conspiring to kill US diplomat, Richard Dwyer, and aiding and abetting the murder of Congressman Ryan. In 1987, he was convicted and sentence to concurrent life sentences, plus 15 years for related offences. He served 18 years and was released in 2002.

CHAPTER 11:

THE BRANCH DAVIDIANS

Victor Houteff, a Bulgarian immigrant to the US, was a Seventh Day Adventist preacher until 1934 when he was defrocked for publishing the book, *The Shepherd's Rod*, which disagreed with the church's interpretation of Chapters 54–66 of the Book of Isaiah. That's why he started his own cult – The Shepherd's Rod, which changed its name to Davidian Seventh-Day Adventists Church in 1942, using the word 'Davidian' after King David.

Houteff believed that there was a hidden meaning in the Bible that would be unlocked by breaking a series of scriptural codes. Once he had done this – surprise, surprise – he discovered that the Apocalypse was at hand and that he, Victor Houteff, had been chosen personally by God to lead a band of the Elect, who would rule the Earth along with Jesus Christ for the thousand years that followed.

DEATH OF A SALESMAN

Earning his living as a part-time washing machine salesman in California, Houteff began to collect a band of followers around him. He bought a ranch near the small town of Waco, Texas, where he established a Bible school called the Mount Carmel Center, which taught his own eccentric interpretation of the scriptures. Houteff's task was to cleanse the world of wickedness, ready for God's coming, but his 40 devoted followers were not the slightest bit fazed when their leader died in 1955 before the last trumpet had sounded.

His wife Florence took over. She made the classic mistake that so many cult leaders have done. She predicted the date of the Apocalypse – in this case 22 April 1959. In 1962, with still no sign of the end of the world, she sold up and another prophet, named Benjamin Roden, took over. He proclaimed what he said was a new message from God, which he outlined in a letter to the remaining Davidians which was signed 'Branch'. This was the new name that Jesus had taken for the final days. Hence the Branch Davidians.

Roden wisely avoided setting a date for the Second Coming. There was still no sign of it when he died in 1978. His wife, Lois Roden, took over, with their son, George Roden, waiting patiently in the wings for his mother to die.

MEMORY MAN

Three years later, 23-year-old Vernon Howell joined the cult. He was the illegitimate son of a Dallas schoolgirl who was just 14 when she gave birth. At school, he was a slow learner, suffering from dyslexia, and he dropped out of school in the ninth grade. He liked sports but failed to develop physically despite his efforts as a bodybuilder. He was also an excruciating heavy metal guitarist. The only thing in the world he was good at was memorizing the Bible. He knew the whole of the New Testament by heart by the time he was 13. He joined the Seventh Day Adventists but was expelled after developing an unhealthy obsession with the pastor's 15-year-old daughter. Then, after a series of menial jobs, fate led him to Waco.

By then, Howell was already an accomplished con man. His comprehensive knowledge of the Bible impressed the Branch Davidians and he threw himself on the mercy of Lois Roden. He confessed he was in the grip of a terrible vice – excessive masturbation.

Howell quickly made himself useful, fixing the ramshackle ranch buildings, repairing cult members' cars and running errands. And they could not fail to be impressed by his knowledge of the scriptures and his religious zeal.

After two years, Howell made his bid for power. Lois Roden was in her late-60s and her grip on the cult was slipping. Howell, now 25, told her that he had had a vision. In it, God had spoken to him, saying they must conceive a child together. Their son would be the last prophet. Even though she was way past the menopause so there was no possibility of conception, Lois was flattered and set about trying to put his prophecy into practice with a will. They became lovers.

This did not go down well with the other Branch Davidians, but Howell used his new position to begin a religious revival and his hellfire-and-damnation sermons put new life into the Davidians. And he told cult members what they wanted to hear – that the Apocalypse was at hand and that they must cleave to him as the new prophet. Lois Roden was no longer required. Howell dumped her and took a 14-year-old bride who bore him two children. He also had sex with other girls in the cult, some as young as ten. The reason for this was simple, he told his flock: he was the ultimate sex machine.

It was all too much for Lois Roden. At the age of 70, she died and her son, George, stepped into her shoes. He rounded on Howell, accusing him of being a worshipper of Satan. His passion for heavy metal music was proof of this. Howell and his offspring were expelled from the cult 'unto the tenth generation'. To everyone's surprise, Howell accepted this. It was, after all, de rigueur for a bona fide prophet to spend time in the wilderness.

LIFE IN EXILE

He left, taking with him 25 cult members, including most of the young blood. They wandered the Midwest in a couple of beat-up trucks, supporting themselves with social security cheques and odd jobs. Surprisingly, they did well enough to send Howell to Israel, confirming him as the chosen leader in the world's last great battle against Satan. Trips to the UK and Australia garnered more followers. Back in the US, he gathered around him a core of mediocre rock musicians. Taking his inspiration from Houteff (if not Charles Manson), Howell saw hidden messages from God encoded in rock songs, especially the blues classic, 'The House of the Rising Sun' – a song about a New Orleans brothel.

Howell had built up a following of over 60, including an inner circle of bodybuilders who called themselves the Mighty Men, when they returned to Waco. In a last-ditch attempt to retain control, George Roden issued what can only be thought of as a satanic challenge. During Halloween 1987, he had the dead body of an 85-year-old Davidian disinterred. Howell could call himself a prophet, Roden said, only if he could raise the corpse from the dead. That, at least, was Howell's tale. Roden said he was just relocating the community's cemetery.

Whatever the case, Roden had played into Howell's hands. He simply accused Roden of being Satan. After all, he had dug up a corpse. What further proof was needed? Howell filed charges against Roden for illegally exhuming a corpse. He was told that the police would need photographic evidence, so Howell set off to the Mount Carmel Center with seven armed men.

In the gunfight that followed, Roden was shot. It was only a flesh wound. Howell and his men were charged with attempted murder but acquitted. Then, Roden murdered Wayman Dale Adair, who had turned up at his house proclaiming that he was the Messiah – a position eagerly sought after in these circles. Roden shot him and hit him on the head with an axe, claiming that Howell had sent Adair to kill him.

A KING TWICE OVER

Roden was adjudged insane and confined to a mental hospital, meaning Howell took over the Mount Carmel Center, which he found had been used as a meth lab. But there is more money in religion than drugs. Now with over 100 followers, Howell set about fortifying the headquarters. Meanwhile, he became obsessed with Madonna – the singer – saying that God had promised her to him.

Vernon Howell changed his first name to David – convenient if you are head of the Branch Davidians – and took the surname Koresh. That was the Hebrew name of the Babylonian King Cyrus, who allowed the Jews to return to Palestine after their exile. The ranch at Waco was renamed Ranch Apocalypse. It would be the battlefield where Armageddon would begin. Satan, Koresh told his followers, would attack them there, probably under the guise of the US Army.

As a king twice over, Koresh's rule became absolute. The sense of paranoia was increased by the nightly harangues about what a hostile place the outside world was plus a diet of war videos. Discipline was rigidly enforced. The Branch Davidians were the Army of God. They now lived under martial law.

Koresh maintained that everything in the commune belonged to him, right down to his followers' underwear. If he demanded they return it in the name of God, they were to strip naked. Of course, all the women belonged to him. God had told the prophet to multiply. His many concubines – picked from among the wives and daughters of his followers – wore the Star of David. Many of the girls he took as lovers were underage. The other men in the compound were denied sex altogether. They lived in single-sex dormitories and, to ease their sexual frustration, they were encouraged to drink heavily. Rationalizing the situation, some men began to view sex as a sinful assault on the physical integrity of women and thanked Koresh for taking that burden upon himself.

David Koresh with his wife Rachel and their two children.

PREPARING FOR BATTLE

While most of his followers were kept locked up in what was now called Ranch Apocalypse, steeling themselves for the battle ahead, Koresh and his Mighty Men were having a good time in the bars and restaurants of downtown Waco. Meanwhile, they were amassing a huge arsenal of weapons, a stockpiling of over 11 tonnes of munitions – including small arms, grenades and tactical weapons such as anti-tank guns.

The US authorities were aware of what was going on thanks to Mark Breault, one of Koresh's original Mighty Men. His wife had already quit the sect and gone back to Australia. Koresh had taken up with a 13-year-old girl, who was lording it over the place. This was too much for Breault. He managed to slip out and phone his wife, who promised to arrange a flight home for him. All that remained to do was to get to Los Angeles where he could catch the plane.

Mark Breault had kept a detailed diary of his time at Waco. Safely back in Melbourne, he and a group of other Australian defectors got together and warned the American authorities that Waco was potentially another Jonestown. Australian TV picked up on the story and devoted an edition of a current affairs programme to the goings-on at Ranch Apocalypse.

On 28 February 1993, the US Bureau of Alcohol, Tobacco and Firearms – the ATF – moved in. Using ladders, they tried to scale the walls of the main building. The first battle lasted nearly an hour. The ATF were hopelessly outgunned. They lost four killed and 24 were wounded. The Davidians lost six, one shot by colleagues 'to put him out of his misery'. Koresh called police headquarters, complaining that the ATF had killed some of his children.

On network TV, the ATF were seen to have bungled the operation, so the FBI took over. They brought in hostage negotiators. But Davidians had stockpiled food, which would keep them going for a year, and they had enough firepower to defend themselves indefinitely. However, the FBI's conciliatory approach showed some success at first. After a week, two older women and 21 children were allowed to leave the compound. But the authorities knew that there were still probably 100 people left inside, at least 17 of them children. The problem was that FBI hostage negotiators had been trained to deal with Muslim fanatics, criminal gangs and politically motivated terrorists. They did not understand the jargon of the apocalyptic Christians. When Koresh talked of the seven seals of the Book of Revelations, the FBI men thought he was a militant environmentalist concerned with the fates of baby seals.

As the siege dragged on, psychological tactics were employed. Spotlights were played on the windows to try and disrupt the cult members' sleep. Loudspeakers blasted the compound with the chanting of Tibetan monks, the screams of dying rabbits and loud rock music. The Davidians simply countered this by blacking out the windows of the ranch and deadening the sound by piling bales of hay against the walls. Weeks of these tactics brought no results and a more gung-ho faction in the FBI began to find favour. Their thinking appealed to the new US Attorney General, Janet Reno. She was concerned about the welfare of the children. She knew they had been sexually abused and was now worried about the insanitary conditions on the ranch.

At 4am on 19 April 1993, after 51 days of siege, two tanks with battering rams rumbled into position. Holes were knocked in the outer walls and tear gas injected into the compound. The Davidians put on their gas masks and prayed. After half an hour, Koresh still refused to negotiate and more gas was pumped in. Three hours later, the process was repeated once more.

Around midday, wisps of smoke were seen. Suddenly, wind whipping across the prairie sent the Ranch up in flames. Then, the ammunition dump went up in a series of huge explosions.

GRISLY END

Eight members of the cult managed to escape the flames, some with their clothes on fire. They were arrested. Over 100 people perished, not all of them voluntarily. Twenty-five of the charred bodies dug out of the ashes of Ranch Apocalypse belonged to children; 12 of them were Koresh's. A two-year-old boy had been stabbed to death and a woman had been shot in the back. Another 17 members died of gunshot wounds. Five of them were children. Koresh had shot himself through the forehead.

Murder and conspiracy charges were laid against the 11 surviving members of the cult. However, the jury found that the ATF had bungled the raid so badly that they were largely responsible for the deaths of their own agents. Five Davidians were found guilty of involuntary manslaughter. Two more were convicted on firearms charges and four walked free.

The faith of the Branch Davidians did not die in the all-consuming flames of Ranch Apocalypse. One member, who was away from the ranch when the siege began, eagerly awaited Koresh's resurrection. Another, who lost a son, two daughters and four grandchildren in the conflagration, continued believing in Koresh's prophecies of the Second Coming. And many believed that the deaths of David Koresh and his followers were avenged in the Oklahoma City bombing in 1995, where 168 were killed. This terrible event took place on the second anniversary of the end of the siege.

CHAPTER 12:

THE MANSON FAMILY

Charles Manson's murderous cult 'The Family' came directly out of that other Family, the Process Church, while his chief lieutenant and hitwoman, Susan Atkins, had connections to Anton LaVey and his First Church of Satan.

Born 'No Name Maddox' in Cincinnati, Ohio, Manson was the illegitimate son of a teenage prostitute. His mother, Kathleen Maddox, found giving her child a first name was just too much effort, so his birth was registered with no name.

She was just 16 and had run away from her home in Ashland, Kentucky to escape her Bible-thumping mother. Manson's father was a drugstore cowboy who called himself Colonel Walker Henderson Scott. He left long before the child's birth and Manson never knew him. But one William Manson married Kathleen briefly and gave her child his surname. Manson also acquired a first name around this time.

But the marriage did not last. Kathleen was not a natural mother and regularly abandoned her child. By the time he was six, she realized that she could not support her son, even on her earnings from prostitution, so she parked him with her mother, while she and her brother, Luther, robbed a gas station. They were caught and jailed for five and ten years respectively.

Manson stayed on with his strict grandparents for a few weeks, then he was farmed out to his mother's sister, Joanne, in McMechen, West Virginia. When Kathleen was paroled, she came back for the boy. Manson was ecstatic.

They began a shiftless existence together, roaming the Midwest. Kathleen, an alcoholic, was always on the fringes of crime and prostitution. Manson never knew whether she was coming home or had been arrested. At any moment, he might be farmed out again. Meanwhile, he was in trouble on his own account for truancy and petty theft.

REJECTED

Then the inevitable happened. Kathleen met a man who wanted her but did not want her child, so she made her son a ward of court and he was sent to the Gibault Home for Boys in Terre Haute, Indiana, where he was beaten regularly and often ran away.

His mother visited him there often and promised he would be back with her pretty soon, but gradually they lost contact. After knocking over a grocery store and stealing $100 (£77), he was sent to Boys' Town, Nebraska, the orphans' home made famous by the 1932 Spencer Tracy movie of the same name. But after four days, Manson and a fellow inmate got a gun, stole a car and committed a series of armed robberies.

Arrested, he was sent to Indiana Boys' School, where he claimed other boys raped him. To protect himself, he pretended to be insane. He escaped 18 times. In 1951, on the run with two others, he robbed a filling station. He was arrested in a stolen car in Beaver City, Utah and charged with driving a stolen car over a state line, a federal offence. He served four years in a federal reformatory, which was a great improvement over children's homes. Manson was found to be illiterate and aggressively anti-social, but he had an IQ of 109.

In November 1954, he was released into the custody of his Aunt Joanne in McMechen. There he met a waitress named Rosalie 'Rosie' Jean Willis. They married in January 1955 and headed for Los Angeles. But he was arrested again for taking a stolen car over the state line into California. He was given five years' probation, but when he failed to appear for other similar offences he was sentenced to three years in Terminal Island Federal Prison in San Pedro near Los Angeles.

Soon afterwards, his wife gave birth to a son. His mother got in touch to tell him that Rosie had taken up with another man. Two weeks before a probation, Manson tried to escape, stealing a car. His parole was denied. Rosie then divorced Manson and disappeared from his life, taking Charlie Junior with her.

Paroled in 1958, he started pimping and was repeatedly arrested under the Mann Act for transporting women across state lines for immoral purposes. He decided that he might have more success forging cheques. He didn't. He was caught passing a stolen cheque for $38 (£30) and absconded to Mexico. When the police caught up with him, he was sentenced to ten years in the federal penitentiary on McNeil Island in Washington State. There, he learnt to play the guitar and took part in hypnosis sessions.

Being small, just 5 ft 2 in (1.57 m), Manson had a hard time in prison. He was raped repeatedly by other prisoners. Many of his assailants were black and this left him with a lifelong racial chip on his shoulder.

Manson was introduced to Scientology in jail. He claimed to be a 'Clear', but there is very little evidence that he took Scientology seriously. What attracted him was the power these ideas gave him over other people. Jail had already taught him to be shifty, cunning and manipulative. The techniques of Scientology were the perfect extension of this, so he was well prepared when he was released on 21 March 1967.

TURN ON, TUNE IN, DROP OUT

When he had gone to jail, it had still been the 1950s and the world had been conservative and dull. When he came out, a new generation was turning on, tuning in and dropping out. Manson was 32 and he headed for the centre of the happening counterculture, the Haight-Ashbury district of San Francisco. He had already heard what was going on in the outside world, but he still could hardly believe his eyes.

'Pretty little girls were running around every place with no panties and bra and asking for love,' he said. 'Grass and hallucinatory drugs were being handed to you on the streets. It was a different world than I had ever been in and one that I believed was too good to be true. It was a convict's dream and after being locked up for seven solid years, I didn't run from it. I joined it and the generation that lived in it.'

One of his first experiences on the outside was attending a Grateful Dead concert, where he dropped a tab of acid. People remember him dancing like a man possessed, then suddenly falling into a trance and curling up in the foetal position. When he left jail, he had just $30 (£22). To make a living, he bought a guitar and began busking. Soon he became something of a star on the streets of Haight-Ashbury. Students also flocked to him on the campus of the University of California and over the bay at Berkeley, another centre of the counterculture. Youth was turning against the establishment and Manson, the institutionalized reject, became flavour of the month.

He soon discovered that the manipulative techniques he had learnt in jail also worked on the long-haired flower children who inhabited southern California. With his hypnotic stare, his unconventional lifestyle and the strange meaningless phrases that sprang to his lips, he was the perfect hippie guru. Along with the Scientological babble he had picked up in jail, he supplemented his New Age lines with the rhetoric that he picked up in becoming a member of the Process Church. Although men were attracted to him, Manson spent most of his energy on recruiting young, middle-class hippie girls who had chicly dropped out.

CHARLIE'S ANGELS

The first female follower was Mary Brunner, a librarian. She was a slim, flat-chested redhead and not very pretty. But she was naive and impressionable, which made her very much Manson's type. Soon, he picked up another girl called Darlene and discovered something new. By sleeping with Mary and Darlene on a strict rota, he found that he could control both of them. He had discovered the power of sex.

When the Process Church moved down to Los Angeles, Mary bought a VW camper and, with his parole officer's approval, they headed south down the coast. On the way, Manson and Brunner sampled communal living – and loving – in the hippie communes that were being established throughout California. Eventually, they reached Los Angeles, where Manson intended to establish himself as a rock superstar.

On Venice Beach in LA, he met another slim redhead, Lynette 'Squeaky' Fromme. She had just had a row with her father and was emotionally vulnerable. Manson brought her back to Mary and had sex with her. The three of them became the nucleus of 'The Family', Manson's hippie cult. Around this central core, a loose collection of hangers-on formed. Among them was a harem of young girls, who were all around ten years younger than Manson. They were each promised a baby in return for their devotion. Added to that, there were several docile young males who did anything Manson told them to do.

WELCOME TO THE FAMILY

At any one time, The Family numbered around 30 to 35. Manson controlled them through acid – LSD – and sex. Every woman who joined the Family had to be initiated by Manson. He gave her a tab of acid and had sex with her for a few hours. He liked to keep the women naked, or at least topless, and choreographed complex orgies, where Manson would control who did what and with whom.

Three members of the Family: Patricia Krenwinkel, Susan Atkins and Leslie van Houten.

An early recruit was Patricia Krenwinkel. A former girl scout, she came from a regular middle-class family. Her expensive education had earned her a good job as a legal clerk at a big insurance company in Los Angeles. She met Manson on Manhattan Beach when she was 21 and abandoned everything to be with him. She ditched her car and walked out of her job without even bothering to pick up her last pay cheque. Leslie Van Houten was just 19 when she dropped out of school. She lived on the streets on a perpetual acid trip until she met Manson. Twenty-year-old Linda Kasabian left her husband and two children, stealing $5,000 from a friend to join The Family in a haze of LSD. Another redhead, Diane Lake, joined after her own parents had dropped out to join the Hog Farm commune. And Ruth Ann Moorehouse, a preacher's daughter, married a hapless bus driver, so that she could leave her parents' home and join The Family.

The woman who brought Satanism to The Family was Susan Atkins. Her real name was Sadie Mae Gutz. At 21, she was a topless dancer and bar-room hustler. Then, she became involved in Anton LaVey's First Church of Satan. Later, she became Manson's closest aide and used acid-fuelled orgies to plant satanist ideas in his followers' receptive minds.

One of the few men in the commune was 23-year-old former high-school football star from Farmersville, Texas, Charles 'Tex' Watson. He had once been an honours student, but in Manson's hands he had become a mindless automaton. Another college drop-out, Bruce Davis, joined them. So did Bobby Beausoleil, former guitarist with the Digger band Orkustra and protégé of underground film-maker Kenneth Anger, author of Hollywood Babylon. Anger was a follower of Crowley and one of LaVey's magic circle. Beausoleil had played Lucifer in Anger's movie, Invocation of My Demon Brother, and taken part in a Black Mass performed on stage at the premier. But Beausoleil spoiled the occasion by ripping off some of Anger's camera equipment. Anger had a locket made with a picture of Beausoleil on one side and a picture of a toad on the other. The inscription read: 'Bobby Beausoleil – who was turned into a toad by Kenneth Anger.' Two years later, Beausoleil was arrested for the Manson murders, while Anger went on to write the best-selling exposé, Hollywood Babylon.

The Family hung around on the fringes of the movie community. With three girls to every man, they were welcome at any party. Often, they would sit in a circle and take acid, indulging in a group trip. Family member, Paul Wilkins, remembered that Manson was always the one who handed out the tabs. He always took less than everybody else. That way he was always in control.

Dennis Wilson of the 1960s Californian band, the Beach Boys, was particularly fascinated by Manson and his lifestyle. The Family freeloaded on him unmercifully. He put them up, fed them and clothed them from his own wardrobe.

ON THE MOVE

The Family quickly grew to the point where the camper could no longer contain them. They moved out to a huddle of shacks around Topanga Canyon. Almost every young hippie drifter on the West Coast passed in and out of The Family at one time or another – Joan 'Juanitta' Wildebush, Juan Flynn, Cathy Gillies, Brook Poston, Sandra Good, T. J. 'the Terrible' Walleman and Steve 'Clem' Grogan. But Kitty Lutesinger, Cathy 'Gypsy' Share and Stephanie Scram became more or less permanent members. There were junior Family members, too. Susan Atkins gave birth to a son, imaginatively named Zezozoe C. Zadfrack, while Mary Brunner had a boy named Valentine Michael after the protagonist in Robert Heinlein's cult 1960s science fiction classic, *Stranger in a Strange Land*.

By and large, the girls in The Family were middle-class drop-outs. Susan Atkins was the only one with a criminal record. The others brought with them money, cars and daddy's credit cards, which provided everything The Family needed to survive. They formed the secret core of The Family. To join, they had to meet Manson's hypnotic gaze and perform seemingly impossible tasks. They were taught to think of themselves as an elite and the outside world as hostile, threatening and beneath contempt. And with their means of support surrendered to Manson, they were completely under his control. Those who did not do what they were told were threatened with expulsion and, occasionally, death.

During his time in Los Angeles, Manson stayed close to the Process Church. When it courted pop stars like John Phillips of The Mamas and the Papas, so did Manson. He certainly saw himself on the satanist wing of the Church. Manson traded the VW camper for a school bus, which he had painted black. It was adorned with the image of the Goat of Mendes/Baphomet painted by Beausoleil. The words 'Holywood [*sic*] Film Production Company' were painted on the side in an attempt to avoid trouble with the police.

When the Process Church broke up, Manson headed for the Mojave Desert. Through contacts in San Diego, The Family got permission to stay out on the Spahn Ranch. This was an old movie set where westerns were shot. It belonged to 80-year-old George Spahn. He was virtually blind. In return for being allowed to stay there, the girls cooked and cleaned for him – and, according to some, provided him with sexual favours. Lynette Fromme later told prosecuting attorney Vincent Bugliosi that she was in love with Spahn and would have married him if he had asked her.

THE DAILY HUSTLE

True to its counter-culture image, The Family fed itself with food thrown out by supermarkets. This was supposed to show how wicked and wasteful the capitalist world was. The effect was marred somewhat by the fact that they picked up the discarded food in a Rolls-Royce. The cult freed itself from the other constraints of straight society by hustling dope, 'borrowing' credit cards and 'liberating' automobiles and other valuables. Family member, Cathy Gillies, rented The Family's second home, the Baker Ranch, using Dennis Wilson's collection of gold records as a deposit.

Surrounded by mewling sycophants, the drug-addled Manson began developing a self-serving philosophy, fuelled by Susan Atkins' satanic studies and his own brushes with Scientology and the Process Church. Atkins managed to convince him that his own name, Manson, was significant. He was Man-son, the Son of Man or Christ. According to her twisted logic, this meant he was also the Devil.

Manson began to see himself as the Gnostic deity, Abraxas – a rooster-headed god with serpent's feet in whom light and darkness, good and evil, are supposed to be unified and transcendent. He saw himself as both Christ and Satan and, naturally, the Apocalypse was at hand. To Manson, that meant a war between blacks and whites.

When the Beatles' *White* album came out, Manson believed that it was a message directed at him and The Family.

'Sexy Sadie' was Susan Atkins, whose real name was Sadie. 'Piggies' sneered at the police and the Establishment and the word became part of The Family's everyday vocabulary. 'Blackbird' was a call for black people to revolt. 'Revolution 9' meant chapter nine of the Book of Revelations to Manson, which talks of the coming of the Apocalypse and the Exterminating Angel.

This was another persona that Manson adopted. One verse in chapter nine reads: 'Neither repent they of their murders, nor of their sorceries, nor of their fornications, nor of their thefts.'

Manson was blissfully unaware that a helter skelter was a harmless British fairground ride. For him, the track 'Helter Skelter' heralded what he saw as the inevitable race war. The blacks would rise up and wipe out the 'piggies' – the forces of law and order, those in authority, the rich and famous and what Manson called 'movie people'. These were the very people he partied with in Los Angeles, who had mysteriously missed his cinematographic potential.

Throughout this cataclysm, Manson and The Family would wait in safety in the desert. Once the blacks were in charge, being inferior he thought, they would find themselves incapable of intelligent rule, so they would naturally turn to him and ask him to take over as world leader. Like Shoko Asahara of Aum Shinrikyo, Manson believed that this apocalyptic scenario needed a helping hand. To this end, Manson tried to recruit biker gangs such as the Straight Satans and, later, turned to violence himself.

BUNGLED MURDER

In the meantime, Manson thought he should try and emulate his heroes, the Beatles, and bring his message to the world through the medium of music. He started writing songs and took one of his compositions to successful West Coast musician, Gary Hinman. It was then that Manson learned that Hinman had recently inherited $20,000 (£15,000). He sent Mary Brunner, Susan Atkins and Bobby Beausoleil to Hinman's house on Old Topanga Canyon Road to steal the money and to murder Hinman for refusing to help make Manson's song top of the charts, which is where Manson, at least, thought it belonged.

The three Family members did as they were told. They went to the house and talked with Hinman for about two hours before Beausoleil lost his patience and pulled The Family's gun, a 9mm Radom pistol. He handed it to Susan Atkins and began searching the house. With Beausoleil out of the room, Hinman tried to escape. Atkins tried to stop him. The gun went off. The bullet ricocheted around the kitchen and embedded itself under the sink. Hearing the shot, Beausoleil ran back, grabbed the pistol and beat Hinman around the head with it. Once he was subdued, they called Manson, who drove over to Hinman's house. Manson took a sword and cut Hinman's ear. He told Beausoleil to find the money. The girls were to clean up Hinman's wound and bring him out to the ranch. Manson then left.

Mary Brunner stitched up Hinman's ear with dental floss, bandaged his other wounds and gave him something to drink. With Hinman tied up on the hearth rug, Beausoleil and Atkins ransacked the house. They could not find any money, but they found two pink slips – the ownership documents for two cars. Under threat of death, Hinman signed them over.

At dawn the next morning, Hinman made another escape attempt. He reached the window and screamed for help. Beausoleil panicked. He grabbed a knife and stabbed him twice in the chest. Hinman was left to bleed to death. Atkins dipped her fingers in his blood and wrote 'political piggies' in blood on the wall. Then, she drew a cat's paw, a crude imitation of the logo of the militant black separatist movement, the Black Panthers. The three of them bundled up the blood-stained bandages and clothes, then tried to wipe their fingerprints off everything they had touched during their long stay in Hinman's house. After that, they left, locking the door behind them. Once outside, they began to worry that Hinman was not dead, so they climbed back in through a window and smothered him for good measure. Then, they hot-wired Hinman's VW van and drove to the Topanga Kitchen, where they celebrated with coffee and cherry cake. Afterwards, they drove back to the Spahn Ranch to tell Manson what they had done.

Hinman's body was found by friends on 31 July 1969, four days after he was murdered. The Los Angeles Sheriff's Office – which deals with crime outside the metropolitan area – was called in. Sergeant Paul Whiteley and Deputy Charles Guenther were assigned to the case. The investigation was not too complicated. The killers had not done a very good job of cleaning up and they found Beausoleil's fingerprints in Hinman's house. On 6 August, they picked up Beausoleil. They found the knife that killed Hinman and a T-shirt drenched in Hinman's blood in Beausoleil's car. He was convicted of murder and sent to jail – without implicating Atkins or Manson.

DEATH SQUAD

This loyalty impressed Manson not at all and he began to plan new acts of violence. Next, he tried to get his song recorded by Terry Melcher, the son of Doris Day who Dennis Wilson of the Beach Boys had introduced him to. Melcher was a big player in the industry but failed to see the potential of Manson's material.

Manson was getting mad. He formed his followers into a death squad. They were dressed in black and were trained in breaking and entering into abandoned buildings. These exercises were known as 'creepy crawlies'. As part of their training, Manson told them they were to kill anyone who stood in their way.

On 8 August 1969, Manson's death squad was despatched to reconnoitre Melcher's remote home on Cielo Drive in Benedict Canyon in the Hollywood Hills. But Melcher had moved. This did not matter to Manson. The people that were seen going in and out of the house were 'movie types'. Their slaughter would act as a warning, so he sent Tex Watson, Susan Atkins, Patricia Krenwinkel and Linda Kasabian to the house armed with a .22 Bluntline Special revolver, a knife and a length of rope.

The house at the end of Cielo Drive was indeed occupied by 'movie people'. Film director Roman Polanski lived there, but he was away shooting a movie in London. His wife, movie star Sharon Tate, who was eight months pregnant, was at home though. Coffee heiress Abigail Folger and her boyfriend, Polish writer Voytek Frykowski, were visiting. So was Sharon Tate's friend, celebrity hairdresser Jay Sebring.

Manson's death squad parked their white and yellow Ford outside 10050 Cielo Drive, while Tex Watson shinned up a telegraph pole and cut the phone lines. Then, Watson, Atkins and Krenwinkel pushed open the wrought-iron gates. Kasabian lost her nerve at the last moment and stayed outside. As the other three went in, a white two-seat Nash Ambassador came down the driveway. It was driven by 18-year-old Steven Parent. He had been visiting the caretaker. Brandishing the .22, Tex Watson leapt into the headlight beams and ordered the driver to stop. He thrust the gun into the car window. Steven Parent begged for his life. Watson pumped four bullets into his chest.

Atkins and Krenwinkel scouted around the house but could not find a way in, so Watson started cutting his way through the screen on the window of an empty room at the front. Once inside the house, Manson's followers found Voytek Frykowski asleep on the couch. He woke to find a .22 in his face and asked the intruders what they wanted.

'I am the Devil,' said Watson. 'I am here to do the Devil's business. Give me your money.'

Watson told Susan Atkins to get some towels to tie Frykowski up. On her way back from the bathroom, she saw Sharon Tate and her other guests talking in the bedroom. She reported this to Watson, who told her to go and get them. Atkins told Sharon Tate and the others that the house was being robbed, but no harm would come to them. But while she was tying them up, Jay Sebring broke free and made a lunge for the gun. Watson shot him in the armpit, then stabbed him four times.

Fearing they were all going to be killed, Voytek Frykowski attacked Watson, who beat him to the ground with the pistol butt. He hit him so hard that the walnut grip of the pistol broke in two. Frykowski staggered to the door, screaming for help. Then, in a frenzy, the girls stabbed Voytek Frykowski to death. There were 51 stab wounds on his body. Frykowski's gallant stand put some fight into the others. Abigail Folger made a break for it, but Krenwinkel caught up with her halfway across the lawn. She was knocked to the ground and Watson stabbed her to death. Sharon Tate begged for her life and that of the unborn child. Despite being a mother herself, Susan Atkins showed no mercy. While Patricia Krenwinkel held Sharon Tate down, Atkins stabbed her 16 times. Tate's mutilated body was then tied to Sebring's corpse. Watson then went around kicking and stabbing the lifeless bodies. The killers spread an American flag across the couch and wrote the word 'pig' on the front door in Sharon Tate's blood. They changed their bloody clothes, collected their weapons and made their way back to the Spahn Ranch, disposing of the evidence on the way.

'I felt so elated,' said Susan Atkins. 'Tired but at peace with the world. I knew this was just the beginning of helter skelter. Now the world would listen.'

Later that night, Manson and another member of The Family returned to Cielo Drive to look for Susan Atkins' knife and clean up. They wiped Steven Parent's car clean, then wiped the house clean of fingerprints with the towel that had been used to tie up Voytek Frykowski. They left it draped over Jay Sebring's face.

Back at the Spahn Ranch, Manson got high on marijuana and read the reports of the murders in the newspapers as if they were movie reviews. To celebrate this great victory, he held an orgy with his female followers.

THE KILLING GOES ON

Two days later, it was clear that the slaughter in Benedict Canyon still had not sparked helter skelter and the Apocalypse, so, on 10 August, Watson, Kasabian, Krenwinkel and Atkins set out again. This time Manson accompanied them. Leslie Van Houten and Steven 'Clem' Grogan came along for the ride. Manson randomly selected a house in the Silver Lake area of Los Angeles. The address was 3301 Waverley Drive. He took his sword and his gun, walked up the drive to a long low house and broke in. The house belonged to 44-year-old grocery store owner, Leno LaBianca, and his 38-year-old wife Rosemary, who ran a fashionable dress shop. They woke to find Manson holding a gun in their faces. He tied them up and told them that they would not be harmed. He only intended to rob them. He took LaBianca's wallet and went outside to the car where the rest of them were waiting. Manson sent Tex Watson, Leslie Van Houten and Patricia Krenwinkel back into the house. He said that he was going to break into the house next door and murder the occupants. Instead, he drove home.

In the LaBianca house, Watson went to work. He dragged Leno LaBianca into the living room and stabbed him four times with a kitchen knife, which he left sticking out of his throat. Using his own knife, Watson then stabbed LaBianca another eight times in the stomach, leaving him to bleed to death with a pillow over his face. Then, Watson and Krenwinkel stabbed helpless Mrs LaBianca 41 times while chanting a murderous mantra. They wanted Van Houten to join in. Reluctantly, she stabbed Mrs LaBianca 16 times in the buttocks, but Mrs LaBianca was already dead.

Watson carved the word 'war' on Leno LaBianca's abdomen. Krenwinkel then stabbed the bodies with a carving fork, leaving it sticking out of Mr LaBianca's stomach. They tied a lamp flex around his neck and put a pillowcase over his face. Using their victim's blood, they wrote revolutionary slogans on the walls – 'death to pigs' and 'rise' in the living room and 'healter [*sic*] skelter' on the refrigerator door. Then, the three killers took a shower together. They had something to eat and went home.

When Sergeant Whitely and Deputy Guenther – the men from the LA Sheriff's Office who had put Beausoleil away – read about the Sharon Tate murders, they saw similarities with the Hinman case, particularly the slogans written on the walls in blood. They knew Beausoleil could not have been involved directly as he was in custody at the time. But they had always suspected he was not alone and they knew that he had hung out with a weird bunch of hippies at the Spahn Ranch. Anyone who had been with Beausoleil on the Hinman murder would be a prime suspect in the Tate killings. Whitely called Sergeant Jesse Buckles, who was on the team handling the Tate case at the Los Angeles Police Department and told him of his suspicions. Buckles pooh-poohed the idea. He did not even report it to his superior officer. After all, the LAPD already thought they had their man.

CITY IN PANIC

The Tate murders were discovered the next morning by Mrs Winifred Chapman, the housekeeper who lived out. The young caretaker William Garretson, who lived in the guest house in the back garden, immediately fell under suspicion. He claimed to have slept through everything. The LAPD did not believe him. They leant on him hard to get him to change his story. But then, when reports of the LaBianca murders came in, Garretson had to be released. Plainly, he could not have killed Mr and Mrs LaBianca while he was in custody.

By this time, Los Angeles was in panic. Poolsides emptied, gun sales soared and security firms were run off their feet. The pressure was on to make a quick arrest.

With no record of Whitely's tip on record, the LAPD's most promising lead was drugs. It was well known that Jay Sebring supplied his clients with marijuana and other drugs. A Polish friend of Voytek Frykowski also told the LAPD that Frykowski, too, was setting up as a drug dealer. However, the Tate case was clearly tied to the LaBianca murders, which were also under the LAPD's jurisdiction. The LaBiancas were a respectable middle-aged couple with no connection to drugs. LaBianca was a keen gambler and racehorse owner. Could he have had Mafia connections? This also led nowhere.

It was not until 15 October, over two months after the Tate murders, that one of the LaBianca team at the LAPD thought of checking out whether any similar cases had been handled by the Los Angeles Sheriff's Office. Unlike Sergeant Buckles and the Tate team, they were immediately interested in the Hinman case. In the meantime, Whitely and Guenther had not been sitting on their hands. On 16 August, the LA Sheriff's Office had raided the Spahn Ranch, looking for stolen cars and credit cards. This made it clear to the killers that their senseless slaughter had not set off helter skelter, the great revolutionary race war, as they had expected. Instead, it had just provoked a police crack-down.

With his predictions in tatters, the Manson cult began to break up.

'When they catch me, it's going to be like feeding me to the lions,' said Manson, exhibiting, for once, considerable insight. 'They're going to put me far away because I have no family, no one that will help me.'

THE COPS' BIG BREAK

Some of The Family fled to the nearby Barker Ranch. But that, too, was raided on 12 October by the local Inyo County Police, who were looking for stolen cars and illegal firearms. They arrested 24 Family members, including Manson himself. It took three days to search the huge ranch properly. When the police approached a dry gully on the outskirts of the ranch, Kitty Lutesinger, who was five months pregnant with Bobby Beausoleil's child, and Stephanie Scram stumbled out. They were exhausted, frightened and begged for police protection.

Since several of The Family members gave the Spahn Ranch as their address, the Inyo County Police phoned the LA Sheriff's Office, whose jurisdiction it was in. Whitely and Guenther had been looking for Kitty Lutesinger, who, as Beausoleil's girlfriend, they had wanted to interview in connection with the Hinman killing. They drove up to see her.

Kitty was eager to help. She told them that she had heard Manson order Bobby Beausoleil and Susan Atkins to go to Gary Hinman's house and get money from him. This tied Manson to the Hinman case. She also said that she had heard other Family members talking about a man being grabbed by the hair and stabbed in the legs. This was not Hinman. He had no wounds on the legs. But it could have been Frykowski.

Susan Atkins was long gone. She had taken off on her own and had turned to prostitution to support herself. By the time

Kitty was interviewed, Atkins was already in custody. When interviewed, Atkins admitted to being at Hinman's house when he was murdered. She was booked on suspicion of murder.

The LAPD already had one of the murder weapons in their possession. The .22 Bluntline Special had been thrown out of the car by the killers on the way back from the LaBianca murders. It was found on a Los Angeles hillside by ten-year-old Stephen Weiss. But the police had just tagged it and filed it away in a manila envelope. Its significance was only recognized after Weiss's father read a description of the gun used in the Tate killings in the *Los Angeles Times*. Meanwhile, the LaBianca team were setting their considerable intelligence-gathering team on gleaning any information they could find on the Manson cult. They even pulled in Danny de Carlo and Al Springer of the Straight Satan bikers gang, who provided a lot of hearsay and

The Family begins its trek on knees from Sunset Strip to the Hall of Justice, 23 June 1971.

circumstantial evidence linking Manson to the murders. And Terry Melcher told the police that Manson had been to 10050 Cielo Drive when he had lived there. The net was closing.

A JAILBIRD SINGS

In jail, Susan Atkins could not keep her mouth shut. She began bragging to her cellmate, Ronnie Howard, and another prisoner named Virginia Graham about the killings. And she said she planned to do unspeakable things to Elizabeth Taylor, Richard Burton, Frank Sinatra, Tom Jones and Steve McQueen when she got out. They grew frightened and reported what she had said to the authorities. Atkins' so-called hit list was released in the papers. A number of the celebrities left town. In the light of her jail-cell confession, Atkins could hardly back down. On 5 December 1969, she testified to a Grand Jury, describing what had really happened at 10050 Cielo Drive on the night of 8 August. And she blamed Manson.

The Manson trial began on 15 June 1970. It lasted for nine-and-a-half months, the longest murder trial in America at that time. The transcript ran to over eight million words. Throughout the entire trial, the jury – seven men and five women – were sequestered. They were kept incommunicado in a hotel and supervised by bailiffs for 225 days. There was a vast amount of evidence to go through and a huge number of witnesses to locate and interview. Tex Watson had gone home to Texas and fought extradition. Manson had his own line in delaying techniques. First, he said he wanted to defend himself. When his request was denied, he rejected the attorneys the court provided one after another. In the end, Manson was defended by Irving Kanarek, who was himself a master of delaying tactics. His notorious obstructionism had once stretched a simple case of theft out until it took up two years of court time.

The defence began by challenging the right of the judge, William Keene, to preside over the case. They won and he was replaced by Judge Charles Older. When the trial was almost over, the newly elected president, Richard Nixon, slipped up. He inadvertently declared Manson guilty. Normally, this would have resulted in the proceedings being declared a mistrial and the whole thing beginning over again. But as the jury were sequestered, it was assumed that they had not heard the president's remark and the trial went ahead.

The Manson trial was unique. Never before in the history of American jurisprudence had a defendant been charged with mass murder by proxy. After all, Manson had not actually killed anyone by his own hand, nor had he been present when the killings were done. Manson's strategy was to maintain his absolute control over his followers, and through them their attorneys. His female followers were still largely in his thrall. Susan Atkins, who had promised to turn state's evidence and testify against Manson, retracted her earlier statements and faced the charges beside him. Inside the court and out, Manson's women pledged to follow him to the end.

On 24 July, Manson appeared in court with a cross carved on his forehead. He had cut it himself with a hacksaw blade. He said nothing but issued a press statement.

'I have Xed myself from your society,' it said.

A few days later, his co-defendants appeared with the same mark on their foreheads. And by the end of the week, The Family women who camped outside the court building had done the same. Manson's X later turned into a swastika.

When Manson turned his back on the judge, so did his followers. Later, he caused uproar by hurling himself at the bench, screaming at the judge that he should have his head cut off. Prosecution attorneys were given bodyguards and walkie-talkies for the duration of the trial. Family members made no direct attack on them, but they did attempt a raid on a gun store that failed. They were apprehended in a bullet-riddled van after a shoot-out with the police. Their plan had been to use the guns to hijack a plane and demand Manson's release.

ARMAGEDDON TIME

During their investigations, the LAPD had spotted the connection between Manson's Family and the Process Church. One former member of the Process Church who was a suspect in two motorcycle murders told them that Manson had used typical Process tactics, but he had lost patience with anyone he could not indoctrinate. He dubbed these the so-called 'Grey Forces' – blacks and the wealthy establishment.

Two members of the Process Church – calling themselves Brother John and Brother Matthew – turned up unannounced to see Deputy District Attorney Vincent Bugliosi during the investigation. They claimed to have been sent by the Church's national headquarters in Cambridge, Massachusetts and delivered a stack of Process literature that officially denied that Manson had anything to do with Robert DeGrimston and the Process Church. But when Bugliosi checked, he discovered that the two men had also visited Manson in jail.

During his interrogation of Manson, Bugliosi asked whether he knew Robert DeGrimston or Robert Moore – Moore being DeGrimston's surname.

'You're looking at him,' Manson said. 'Moore and I are one and the same.'

Bugliosi later drew parallels between the teachings of Manson and the Process, particularly their view that it was their duty to help instigate an imminent and violent Armageddon.

FINAL RECKONING

Manson's strategy of letting his acolytes take the rap failed. Linda Kasabian took the stand as a witness for the prosecution. She said she loved Manson, then told the court everything she knew about the murders. She had been outside 10050 Cielo Drive during the Tate killings and she had heard other Family members talk about the murder of the LaBiancas. More damningly, she addressed Manson from the stand.

'I am not like you, Charlie,' she said. 'I can't kill anyone.'

Manson's defence had tried to establish Tex Watson as the evil genius behind the murders. But when he finally arrived from the Texas jailhouse where he had been held during the lengthy extradition battle, the jury saw a good-looking, clean-cut, square-jawed, all-American boy – not anyone's picture of an evil genius at all.

Watson told the court: 'Charlie called me over behind a car. He said for me to take the gun and the knife and go up to where Terry Melcher used to live. He said to kill everyone in the house as gruesomely as possible.'

In what amounted to a threat, Manson told the jury: 'You say there are just a few in my Family. There are many, many more, coming in the same direction. They are running in the streets, and they are coming right at you.'

Then he taunted the jury with a chilling half-truth.

'I've killed no one,' he said. 'I've ordered no one to be killed. These children who come to you with their knives, they're your children. I didn't teach them – you did.'

But no one was fooled. Everyone knew who was responsible. Manson, Beausoleil, Atkins, Krenwinkel, Van Houten and Grogan were all sentenced to death in the gas chamber. Manson was not even afraid.

'My faith in me is stronger than all your armies, government, gas chambers or anything you may want to do to me,' he said.

In some ways, he was right. Before the sentence could be carried out, the death penalty was abolished in California. Manson and his followers had their sentences commuted to life imprisonment.

Former Family member, Lynette Fromme, made a half-hearted attempt to get Manson out. In 1975, she pulled a gun on President Gerald Ford. But she did not pull the trigger and succeeded only in putting Manson back in the headlines again.

Manson constantly asked for parole. He did it, not because he had a chance of getting out, but because it got him publicity. He revelled in his image as Satan incarnate and boasted that he had been responsible for 35 other murders. He died in jail in 2017. At the time of the trial, Manson's connections to the Process Church became quite well known and Process suffered something of a backlash. Members gave up their distinctive black attire and wore grey leisure suits instead and DeGrimston dropped out of sight. In an effort to save the Church in the US, Mary MacLean changed its name, dropped the Lucifer and Satan wings, then dropped out of sight herself. According to retired captain Dale Griffis of the Tiffin, Ohio, Police Department, she changed her name to Circe and opened an occult shop in Toledo, Ohio. She bought a tract of real estate adjacent to a location said to be the site of satanic rituals involving human sacrifice. In 1985, law enforcement officers dug up the site and, although some ritualistic paraphernalia was found, there was no evidence of human remains. However, the occult shop in Toledo closed soon after and Circe mysteriously disappeared.

Meanwhile, a number of other members of the Process Church returned to England and, by 1988, they were proselytizing their murderous creed as if they had never been away.

CHAPTER 13:

THE TWENTY-TWO DISCIPLES OF HELL

There were ties between the Manson Family, the Process Church and another famous killer. In 1976 and 1977, the 'Son of Sam' terrorized New York. He was given the nickname by the newspapers after he sent a note to the police saying that he had been ordered to kill by his father Sam, who was a vampire.

In a letter to *Daily News* columnist Jimmy Breslin, he identifies himself as 'Sam's creation'. When the *Daily News* published the letter, they withheld the postscript, which read:

'HERE ARE SOME NAMES TO HELP YOU ALONG. FORWARD THEM TO THE INSPECTOR FOR USE BY THE NCIC: "THE DUKE OF DEATH", "THE WICKED KING OF WICKER", "THE TWENTY-TWO DISCIPLES OF HELL", JOHN "WHEATIES" – RAPIST AND SUFFOCATER OF YOUNG GIRLS. PS: J.B. PLEASE INFORM ALL THE DETECTIVES WORKING THE SLAYINGS TO REMAIN.'

The police said that they did not want this section released because they did not want the public to know about the NCIC – the National Crime and Information Center. But perhaps the real reason was the satanic undertones in the list of names he produced. The 'Wicked King of Wicker' is presumably the king of 'Wicca', or 'The Craft', a modern-day pagan cult. And the 'Twenty-Two Disciples of Hell' certainly sounds like a satanic organization. Then there was John 'Wheaties' who was supposed to be the 'rapist and suffocater [*sic*] of young girls'. 'Wheaties' had quotation marks around it, as if a nickname, but investigations led nowhere.

One of the problems of capturing the Son of Sam was that, although the killer always used the same gun, a .44, his description varied wildly, which indicated that there could have been more than one person involved in the killings. Indeed, the walls of his apartment in Yonkers were daubed with satanic graffiti.

INCONSISTENCIES

In August 1977, David Berkowitz was arrested. He pleaded guilty to all the Son of Sam murders and was sentenced to 365 years in prison. And that seemed to be the end of that.

However, not everyone was satisfied. Investigative reporter, Maury Terry, spotted inconsistencies in Berkowitz's story. A number of the descriptions given did not match Berkowitz, neither in height nor hair colour, although they were consistent with each other. And in one of the killings, Berkowitz could not have acted alone if all the witnesses were telling the truth. Terry interviewed them again and was convinced they were. What's more, in another letter to the *New York Post*, dated 19 September 1977, Berkowitz indicated that he had accomplices. 'There are other Sons out there, God help the world,' he said.

Terry was fascinated by the name 'Son of Sam'. Berkowitz's real father was named Tony. He had a stepfather, but his name was Nathan. There was only one Sam in the case. His name was Sam Carr, a neighbour of Berkowitz's in the Bronx, who suspected Berkowitz of being responsible for a long campaign of harassment. His house had been petrol-bombed. Shots had been fired through the window and Carr's dog had been shot. Berkowitz had complained to other neighbours that Carr was spying on him.

Strangely, although Carr's house was visible from Berkowitz's sixth-floor apartment, they said they had never met, though Berkowitz claimed to have received his murderous instructions from Carr's dog.

Carr had two estranged sons, John and Michael. He also had a daughter named Wheat. Terry remembered the John 'Wheaties' who was the 'rapist and suffocater of young girls' in the Breslin letter. Descriptions of John Carr also matched those given by Son of Sam witnesses that did not fit Berkowitz.

David Berkowitz, the 'Son of Sam'.

DEVIL WORSHIP

Terry was also interested in Berkowitz's seeming obsession with dogs. He discovered that in Walden, New York, about an hour's drive from Berkowitz's home in Yonkers, 85 Dobermans and Alsatians had been found skinned during the year of the Son of Sam killings. More dead dogs had been found in a wooded part of Untermyer Park in Yonkers. A local teenager said that devil-worshippers held ceremonies there. Could Berkowitz have been involved in a satanic cult – the Twenty-Two Disciples of Hell, perhaps? The police dismissed the idea, though Berkowitz doubled down by naming two members of the cult – John and Michael Carr. They were the sons of Sam Carr.

In October 1978, when Terry eventually traced John Carr, it was too late to ask him about any of this. He had been shot dead in the small town of Minot, North Dakota. His body had been found in the bedroom of his girlfriend, Linda O'Connor, with a bullet through the roof of the mouth and a rifle beside the body. The coroner's verdict was suicide, but the police believed he had been murdered.

John Carr was born in Yonkers, New York, on 12 October 1946. He shared his birthday with occultist Aleister Crowley. After leaving Catholic school, Carr joined the US Air Force. He was stationed in Korea and served 12 years. In 1972, he returned to the US and was stationed in Minot. He was discharged in 1976, allegedly for drug addiction. In 1976 and 1977, he went to hospital three times with overdoses and he had a reputation as a drug dealer and heavy drinker. He was in New York around the time of five of the eight Son-of-Sam attacks, including those where witnesses had given a description that matched his.

In late January 1978, Carr again drove the 1,500 miles (2,400 km) from Minot to New York, saying that he was going to stay in the city for a long time. But within two weeks, he called his girlfriend and told her that the police were after him. On 14 February, he flew back to Minot. He rented a post office box, opened a bank account and enquired about the continued payment of a disability allowance he received for a service injury – hardly the actions of a man contemplating suicide. Two days later, he was dead.

Mysteriously, on the skirting board by the body, the letters 'S.S.N.Y.C.' were scrawled in blood. A man who has blown the top of his head off with a rifle bullet seldom has time to write things in his own blood. Terry deduced that Carr had been beaten to the ground by his assailants, then his killer, or killers, had gone to search for his gun to kill him, leaving him time to write the message. The letters 'S.S.N.Y.C.', Terry concluded, stood for 'Son of Sam, New York City'. Carr also had the figures '666' written in blood on his hand. 666 was the number of the Beast in the Book of Revelations and was used as a satanic pseudonym by Aleister Crowley. The police in Minot also discovered that Carr was connected to a number of local occult groups and his girlfriend said that, when Carr had seen news of Berkowitz's arrest for the Son-of-Sam shootings on TV, he had said, 'Oh, shit.'

CASE RE-OPENED

Up to this point, Terry had been dismissed as a conspiracy theorist. But John Santucci, the District Attorney of Queens, began to believe that there was something to Terry's investigation. He re-opened the case. It was soon discovered that, far from being the classic psychotic loner, Berkowitz had a wide circle of friends. Chief among them was John 'Wheaties', Carr's brother, Michael. In 1975, the year before the killings started, Michael, a drug addict who hung around Berkowitz's apartment block, invited Berkowitz to a party. The guests included John Carr and other members of the Twenty-Two Disciples of Hell, the satanic group Berkowitz referred to in the Breslin letter. In due course, Berkowitz moved to Yonkers, to within 200 yards of the home of Sam Carr, where Michael Carr then lived.

Since then, Michael Carr had moved out and, by the time he could be traced, he too was dead. In the early hours of 4 October 1979, Michael Carr's car ran into a streetlight at 75 miles an hour (120 kph) as he drove towards Manhattan. There were no skid marks and his sister, Wheat, who worked for the Yonkers Police Department, was convinced he had been forced off the road, or

Maury Terry (from the Netflix documentary *The Sons of Sam*).

that one of his tyres had been shot out. According to Terry, he had been an active member of the Church of Scientology.

None of the other members of the Twenty-Two Disciples of Hell were found. But the postman who delivered Berkowitz's letters in Yonkers killed himself. His name was Andrew Dupay and he was a young married man. In the month before Berkowitz was arrested, he was noticeably worried. Then on 20 September 1977, five weeks after Berkowitz's arrest, he and his wife were bathing their two baby daughters when Dupay excused himself, went down to the basement of his home and blew his head off with a shotgun. A neighbour said that Dupay had said that he had learned something on his rounds that had frightened him. One of Terry's informants said that Dupay knew both Carr and Berkowitz and had killed himself because threats had been made against his family.

On 7 January 1978, the body of Mary Hirschmann was found on a vacant lot in Queens. She had been strangled and stabbed. Her husband's body had been found the day before, riddled with bullets, in the East Fishkill district of north Yonkers. He had mystical figures tattooed on his body.

On 16 December 1979, abstract painter Howard Green and his girlfriend, Carol Marron, were found beaten to death over the Hudson River from New York in New Jersey. Their apartment on DeKalb Avenue in Brooklyn was filled with satanic paraphernalia and Carol had been making enquiries about joining Crowley's OTO [Ordo Templi Orientis, or Order of the Temple of the East].

COCK-AND-BULL STORY?

The most unexpected witness in Santucci's new investigation was Berkowitz himself. In February 1979, he had called a press conference and announced that his story about Sam Carr's dog had been concocted in the hope of an insanity plea. But court-appointed psychiatrists had passed him sane. Now, a year after being incarcerated in Attica Correctional Facility, he confessed that was the case. In prison, he had become a prolific letter-writer and his letters revealed that, even before his arrest, he had stage-dressed his apartment to look like that of a lunatic.

In a letter to a priest in California, he wrote:

'I really don't know how to begin this letter, but at one time I was a member of an occult group. Being sworn to secrecy or face death, I cannot reveal the name of the group, nor do I wish to. The group contained a mixture of satanic practices, which included the teachings of Aleister Crowley and Eliphas Levi [a 19th-century occultist]. It was (and still is) blood orientated, and I am certain you know what I mean. The Coven's doctrines are a blend of ancient Druidism, the teachings of the Secret Order of the Golden Dawn, Black Magick, and a host of other unlawful and obnoxious practices. These people will stop at nothing, including murder. They have no fear of man-made laws or the Ten Commandments.'

Berkowitz made other disturbing references in his letters. Shortly after the Son-of-Sam shootings had begun, he applied for a job in a dog pound. The pay was not good, but Berkowitz said: 'There was another way in which I was getting paid. Someone needed dogs. I guess you understand what I'm trying to say.' Terry's investigation again proved that Berkowitz was telling the truth.

SATANIC KILLING

Then Berkowitz dropped a bombshell. In 1979, he ripped a chapter out of a standard work on satanism and witchcraft, claiming that it referred to satanic practices employed by Charles Manson and his Family. Sending it to the police in North Dakota, he wrote in the margin: 'Call Santa Clara's Sheriff's office. Please ask the sheriffs what happened to Arlis Perry.' He went on to say that Arlis Perry had been 'hunted, stalked and slain. Followed to California, Stanford Univ'.

Stanford University is in Santa Clara County. A 19-year-old student called Arlis Perry had been horribly murdered in the church in Stanford University at midnight on 12 October 1974. She had only been in California a few weeks. Her body was naked from the waist down. Her legs were spread and a 30-inch candle was rammed into her vagina. Her arms were crossed over her chest and another candle was put between her breasts. Her jeans lay inverted over her legs. She had been beaten, strangled and stabbed behind the ear with an ice pick. Little of this was made public until 1988, but Berkowitz knew details of the murder that had been withheld. He even cut out a picture from a newspaper that he said resembled Arlis Perry.

The picture of Perry that had appeared in the newspapers was from her school yearbook. But Berkowitz picked out a picture that looked much more like Arlis Perry on the night she died. At the very least, he had seen a picture of the murder, Terry maintained. He said that it was performed by a group of Satanists in California, linked to Charles Manson. Berkowitz said that Arlis Perry had once been a member of the group and had tried to leave.

Terry noted that some of the Son-of-Sam killings were performed with a ruthless efficiency, while others with inept and bungling. He concluded that Berkowitz had committed only three of the Son-of-Sam murders. The victims had been women, who had known about the Twenty-Two Disciples of Hell, or had offended members. Terry believes that the other murders were committed by John Carr and a woman member of the Twenty-Two Disciples who had disguised herself with a balaclava. He also thinks that at least two of the killings were filmed.

On 10 July 1979, Berkowitz was slashed with a razor by another inmate in his maximum-security block. The cut needed 56 stitches and nearly killed him. He would not say who attacked him. Later, he said that it was an attempt by a satanic cult to make him live up to his vow of silence. Maury Terry claimed that the cult was 'a Process offshoot with OTO crossover' and even named its leader. He was Roy Alexander Radin, a tycoon who had earned his money in show business. He moved to California in 1982. But by the time Terry tracked him down, yet again, it was too late. Radin had been murdered on Friday, 13 May 1983. His body was found dumped in Death Valley – Charles Manson's old stamping ground. A defaced Bible was found nearby. Could Radin have been Grand Chingon of the Four P Movement described by the satanic cannibal, Stanley Dean Baker?

DID BERKOWITZ ACT ALONE?

Although Roy Radin and John and Michael Carr were dead and David Berkowitz was locked up, Terry reckoned that the other members of the Twenty-Two Disciples of Hell are still at large and active.

In the early 1990s, Berkowitz claimed that he had joined a satanic cult in 1975, around the time he was hanging out with Michael Carr. Then he announced that he had killed only three of the Son of Sam victims and had only fired the gun in the first attack and the sixth. In every incident, he was involved with other members of the cult in the killings. He said he could not name the others – with the exception of John and Michael Carr – without putting his family in danger.

One of them, he said, was a woman. On 23 October 1976, she had pulled the trigger in the shooting of 20-year-old security guard, Carl Denaro, and student Rosemary Keenan, 18. They were wounded but survived. This was because his accomplice was unfamiliar with the powerful recoil of the .44 Bulldog.

He also said that five members of the cult had been involved in the shooting, on 30 January 1977, of 26-year-old secretary Christine Freund and her fiancé, 30-year-old bartender, John Diel. The actual shooter, Berkowitz said, was a prominent cult member brought in from outside New York and known only as Manson II.

The gunman in the killing of secretary, Stacy Moskowitz, and clothing salesman, Robert Violante, both 20, on 31 July 1977, came from North Dakota, he said. John Carr had been living in North Dakota and Berkowitz's note about the Arlis Perry case was sent to the police there. Berkowitz also admitted to being influenced by literature from the Process Church. When he was arrested, he had been carrying a list of telephone numbers, including the number for the Fort Harrison Hotel, the Church of Scientology's headquarters in Clearwater, Florida.

'I am convinced,' said Terry. 'The evidence is quite clear that an organized satanic group – be they genuine Process, official OTO or a subgroup resulting from internal schisms – exists and carries out illegal rituals. It is beyond doubt that some of these involve murder. And this isn't just an American problem. The whole thing started up again in Britain with Aleister Crowley and he exported it to the United States. This is a multinational problem and England isn't exempt.'

He spelt out his findings in his book, *The Ultimate Evil*, and the Netflix documentary, *The Sons of Sam*.

In 2018, the police matched DNA found on Arlis's jeans to that of Stanford University security guard, Stephen Crawford, who then shot himself. He had no known links to the Process Church, David Berkowitz, Charles Manson's Family or any other cult.

CHAPTER 14:

KILLER CULTS

THE ORDER OF ASSASSINS

The most famous killer cult in history was the Order of Assassins. They were founded in Daylam, Iran by Hasan-i Sabbah, who died in 1124. He was the leader of the Nizari Isma'ili, a religio-political Shia sect, which existed from the 11th to the 13th century. In its early years, it considered murdering its enemies a religious duty.

The Arabic name means 'hashish smoker', referring to the Assassins' alleged practice of taking hashish to induce ecstatic visions of paradise before setting out to face martyrdom. The historical existence of this practice is doubtful. The stories told by Marco Polo and other travellers told of luxuriant gardens, where drugged devotees were given fine food and beautiful women as a foretaste of eternal bliss. These are not confirmed by any known Isma'ili source. Indeed, the sect inhabited dusty hill forts and the presence of women was forbidden during military campaigns.

In 1094, with some Persian allies, Hasan-i Sabbah seized the hill fortress of Alamut in Daylam in Iran. Opposing the growing empire of the Seljuq Turks, who were Sunni, he established a small Nizari Isma'ili state, which he defended by sending assassins into enemy camps and cities to murder the generals and statesmen who opposed him. These were known as *fida'i* or devotees who offer their life for others or in the service of a particular cause.

The Nizari Isma'ili killing of Nizam al-Mulk in 1092.

FANATICAL LEADER

Educated in Cairo, Hasan was known for his ascetic and austere religious lifestyle, reading, writing and administering. He expected devotees to be true believers, exhibiting absolute faith. He was equally tough on his own family. When one of his sons was accused of murder and another of drunkenness, he had them both executed.

The cult's most important follower was Rashid ad-Din Sinan, who headed the Order of the Assassins from 1162 until his death in 1193. During the Third Crusade, headquarters were a fortress at Masyaf, in northern Syria, and he was known to Westerners as the Old Man of the Mountain. Feared for his practice of sending his followers to murder his enemies, he made several attempts on the life of the sultan Saladin, who was a Sunni Kurd.

Saladin responded by besieging Masyaf. One night, Saladin awoke to see a figure leaving his tent. He found a poisoned dagger and a note that warned him to lift the siege or face death. Saladin realized that the figure he'd seen leaving his tent had been Sinan himself. Unable to subdue the Assassins, he made peace with Sinan to prevent him aligning with the crusaders. Two Assassins murdered Conrad of Monteferrat, who had been elected King of Jerusalem. But, under torture, one of the assassins claimed that this was done at the behest of the king of England, Richard the Lionheart.

Assassin power came to an end when the Mongols invaded Persia. One by one, their castles fell until, in 1256, Alamut was overrun. The Syrian fortresses were eventually subjugated by the Mamaluk sultan Baybars I, who installed Mamaluk governors. The Mamaluks are thought to have taken on the Assassins with a fixed fee per murder and a payout to their children if they were killed. However, there is no recorded activity after the 13th century. Nonetheless, the Nizari Isma'ili sect still exists, with the Aga Khan as its Imam.

THE CULT OF KALI

The British Raj stamped out the murderous cult of Kali in India. Kali is the Hindu goddess of destruction and bloodshed. Originally, humans were sacrificed to her, but in modern times a goat was substituted. At the height of her cult, in the 18th and 19th centuries, so many goats were sacrificed day and night that rivers of blood cascaded down the steps outside her temple at Vindhyachal, near Mirzapur on the Ganges.

Among her followers were the Thuggee, or Thugs, a secret society of stranglers who terrorized travellers in northern India for hundreds of years. Their principal activity was strangling travellers and stealing their possessions. But the Thuggee did not consider themselves thieves. Each murder was carried out according to a rigid ritual and the victim was considered a sacrifice to Kali. Strangulation was a holy act, because they believed Kali herself had strangled another demon, Rukt Bij-dana, at the dawn of time. The sweat falling from her brow formed into two men and they – and their male offspring – were sent out into the world to strangle others.

The Thuggee worked in gangs, who would make an annual pilgrimage to Vindhyachal to hand over a share of their loot to the priests of Kali. In return, they would be given the blessing of Kali and her protection.

Out on the road, they would seek out a group of travellers, befriend them and join their caravan. Then, when the portents

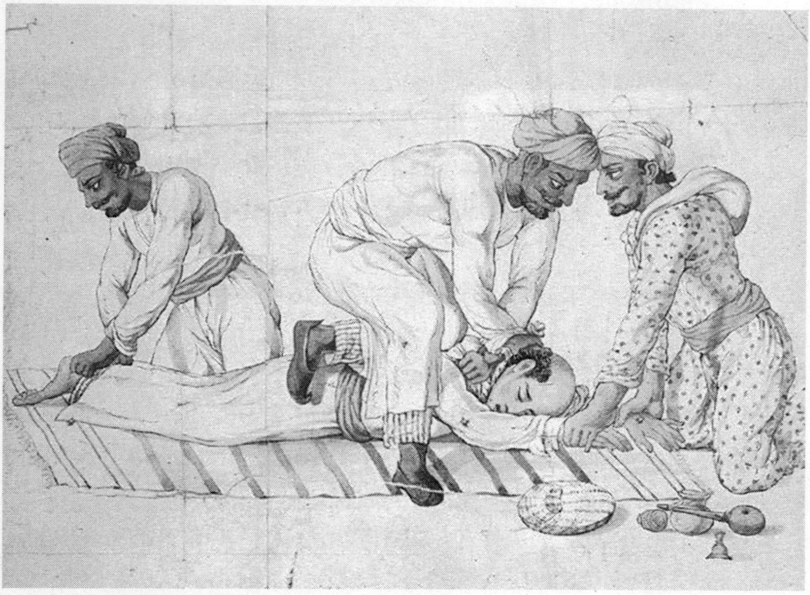

Thuggee attack a traveller, c. 1830s.

were right, they would strangle them. This was done using a *rumal*, a yellow handkerchief with a silver rupee tied in the middle as a garrotte.

The body was then ritually mutilated, and either buried or thrown down a well. Any of the victim's possessions that had no cash value were burned. The rest, along with saleable children, were taken as the Thuggee swiftly moved on.

Selling stolen goods was not the motive for the killers, the Thuggee maintained. It was the munificence of Kali, provided so that they could carry on killing in her honour.

A STRANGLER'S LIFE

The son of a Thuggee would follow his father into the craft, beginning as a scout, then graduating to become a grave-digger. In due course, he would become an assistant strangler, then a strangler himself. A youth's first murder would be celebrated as a rite of passage. There would be elaborate ceremonials involving the *kussee* or sacred pick-axe, said to be a tooth from the mouth of Kali and without which no murder could be sanctified.

The Thuggee had a secret language and other rites and rituals that surrounded their murders. There were special sacred groves, where the strangling was carried out. They would bury their victims in a circular pit, with the corpses packed tightly around a central core of earth to prevent jackals digging up the bodies. After each murder, the Thuggee would consume a lump of consecrated yellow sugar – or *goor* – which they believed sanctified them. Once a man had tasted *goor*, it was said, he would become a Thuggee, no matter how rich or squeamish he was.

When the British first came to India, they tolerated the Thuggee. It was a local custom and should be respected, old India hands said. The Indians themselves maintained an *omertà*.

The Thuggee permeated all levels of society and no one felt safe from the wrath of Kali. The Thuggee maintained that they had a mystical partnership with the tiger.

'Those who escaped the tiger fell into the hands of the Thugs,' said one. 'And those who escaped the Thugs were devoured by tigers.'

It was estimated that the Thuggee killed up to 40,000 people a year. Individual Thuggee boasted more than a thousand victims and gangs had up to 300 members. In 1830, one gang murdered 108 people in just three months.

THE CRACK-DOWN

This tolerant attitude towards the Thuggee ended in 1834, when Lord William Bentinck was appointed Governor-General. With reforming zeal, he was determined to crack down on female infanticide and *sati* – the practice of a widow immolating herself on the funeral pyre of her dead husband. He also swore to put an end to what he called 'the most dreadful and extraordinary secret society in the history of the human race' – the Thuggee.

He appointed Captain William Sleeman Commissioner for the Suppression of Thuggee and Dacoity (the anglicized version of the Hindi word for banditry). With headquarters at Saugor, now Sagar, he ran an intelligence operation, tracking Thuggee activities on a ten-foot-square map.

Sleeman was ruthless. Convicted Thuggee were branded with the words 'Convicted Thug' on the shoulder and 'Thug' was tattooed on their eyelids. Then, they would be hanged. Those willing to inform on other Thuggee would be spared but never freed. Taking them at their word, Sleeman argued that 'like tigers, their thirst for blood would never be appeased'.

Sleeman found Thuggee everywhere. They worked as senior aides to Indian rajahs and as the trusted servants of British officials. Many served in the Indian Army and several worked for British Intelligence.

The Thuggee felt no remorse at what they had done and were proud to have followed in the footsteps of their fathers and grandfathers. One man, who had personally killed 931 times, explained to Sleeman the joy of outsmarting travellers and killing them was an exquisite pleasure. When Sleeman accused him of thieving, he was shocked.

'Thieving? Never,' he said. 'If a bankers' treasure were before me and entrusted to my care, though in hunger and dying I would spurn to steal. But let a banker go on a journey and I would certainly murder him.'

Sleeman's methods were so effective that the Thuggee realized that their goddess Kali was losing the battle with the Christian God of Sleeman and Bentinck. They blamed themselves. They had been neglecting her worship, so she had withdrawn her protection.

By 1841, the Thuggee had been almost completely stamped out. Several thousand Thuggee had been tried and hundreds hanged. The rest were imprisoned or transported to penal settlements on the Andaman Islands. The less bloodthirsty were held in Jubbulpore and were taught weaving, carpet-making, carpentry and bricklaying. Nevertheless, the Criminal Tribes Act was passed in 1871. This was repealed on Indian independence in 1947.

However, in 1970, a bus driver and his father were accused of sacrificing a ten-year-old boy to Kali. Villagers claimed that they felt giddy after eating a sacred chapatti, which the accused had distributed after they had worshipped the goddess.

POLITICAL CULTS

Cults are not restricted to off-the-wall whacky religious beliefs. Minority political movements can operate in the same way, usually with one charismatic leader laying down the law with a bunch of docile followers doing what he – and it usually is a he – says without question. You may argue that's what happens in mainstream politics anyway, but it is hardly the same if the majority of a nation votes that way – or, in the case of a dictator, the whole apparatus of the state enforces compliance.

CHAPTER 15:

COLONIA DIGNIDAD

Colonia Dignidad – 'Dignity Colony' – was an agricultural colony of displaced Germans set up in southern Chile in the aftermath of World War II. In 1961, it was taken over by fugitive paedophile and preacher Paul Schäfer, a follower of the teachings of William Branham who started Jim Jones off on his murderous ministry.

Schäfer ruled the enclave with an iron fist. Married couples were separated and their children taken away from them and sexually abused, but the sect escaped investigation initially because of its purported charitable status. However, when General Augusto Pinochet took over Chile as military dictator in 1973, it also served as a detention centre where opponents of the regime were tortured. It was also reportedly used as a haven for former Nazis escaping retribution in Europe.

SEXUAL ABUSE

Paul Schäfer was born into a Lutheran family in Troisdorf, Germany in 1921. He was a member of the Hitler Youth and served in the Luftwaffe during World War II. After the war, he became a welfare worker for children and a lay preacher at the Evangelical Free Church, but he was dismissed after being accused of sexually abusing boys in his care. He then set off around Germany as an itinerant preacher.

When Branham toured Europe in 1955, Schäfer was one of his security detail and they became friends. They both believed in a strict adherence to the Bible, a woman's duty to obey her husband and racial purity. He also fell for Branham's Latter Rain doctrine, which was seen as totalitarian and misogynistic with an apocalyptic message, perfect for brainwashing all those who were willing to follow it. After hearing one of Branham's sermons, Schäfer claimed to have experienced 'a healing' and began to preach that all sin and illness was the result of demonic possession.

He ran a children's home and orphanage in Gronau, working with at-risk children. His followers were largely war widows and their children, who were refugees from Soviet-occupied East Prussia. Like Branham, Schäfer insisted that his followers were the only faithful ones. Again, he was accused of sexual abuse. This time, he was charged and an arrest warrant was issued. He fled, taking his followers to the Middle East where he relocated his congregation. There, he had contact with the Chilean ambassador, who invited him to Chile, which was one of the South American countries that were eager to provide a safe haven for Germans on the run.

In 1961, he resurfaced at *Sociedad Benefactora y Educacional Dignidad* (Charitable and Educational Society 'Dignity'), a utopian experiment which was set up on a ranch near Parral in the mid-1950s to promote and preserve German culture, language and education. Its residents wore traditional dress – lederhosen and dirndls – and lived in a Bavarian-style village, working in mills, factories, farms and the hospital that the community had built. Local Chileans were treated there for free, earning the cult generous government subsidies.

Schäfer and ten of his followers began preparing the ranch for his congregation. In 1963, 230 arrived, followed by another 15 families in 1966 and 1973, spurred on by Branham's prediction that there would be a nuclear war. South America was thought to be the best place to survive it. Schäfer steered the community towards the principles espoused by William Branham and the society gradually evolved into the Colonia Dignidad cult. He preached an apocalyptic creed, which incorporated anti-Semitism and anti-communism. Former inmates said he was an unlikely-looking Messiah, with his long, grey hair and glass eye, the result of an accident in his youth.

Barbed wire surrounds the Colonia Dignidad compound, 1990.

SLAVERY AND SUFFERING

Like other recruits, Helmut Schaffrick and his wife, Emi, had sold their house in Germany on the promise of a new life in Chile. They handed over the equivalent of $22,500 (£17,500) to Schäfer, who said it was enough for a temporary stay.

'But they were tricked,' said their son, Horst. 'They thought they would build a place where they would do good works and live like good Christians. They found nothing but slavery and suffering.'

Some 300 people lived in the 70 square mile (181 square km) enclave in the foothills of the Andes, surrounded by barbed wire, barricades, roadblocks, searchlights, hidden cameras and microphones. Guard dogs were trained to hunt escapees and sensors were hidden under rocks surrounding the property. Schäfer's excuse for this was that the left-wing government of Salvador Allende, which came to power in 1970, planned to dispossess them. But they would be ready. Knowing that containers for charitable organizations were not checked by customs, Schäfer smuggled in weapons from Germany, including machine guns, which were copied in the colony's machine shops. He also invited Roberto Thieme, the leader of the neo-Fascist group *Patria y Libertad*, to visit and offered to let him use the colony as a base for a coup against Allende.

Occupants of the colony endured tough punishment, constant surveillance and brutal working conditions. Men were made to work in the mills and factories, women in the stables, kitchens and hospital. They sometimes worked for up to 16 hours a day. Heinz Kunz, a former settler who left the group in the 1980s, said: 'I can't begin to tell you how hard he made me work… 12 hours straight with nothing but bread or tea.'

People were subjected to beatings, electric-shock therapy and drugs. Youngsters were given sedatives to control them, or electric shocks to their genitals to keep them in line. After having a child, couples were then forced to live apart in single-sex dormitories and members were allowed few personal possessions. Newborn babies were taken from their mothers and raised by 'nurses' who were known as 'aunts'. Once separated from their parents, they were kept in a children's house where Schäfer was *Der Permanente Onkel* ('the Permanent Uncle'). Without the protection of their parents, he was free to sexually abuse them. The community was totally isolated, with only a select few given access to news from the world outside.

Some people eventually managed to escape, bringing with them stories of the terrible conditions in the colony. In 1966, teenage fugitive, Wolfgang Kneese, managed to find asylum in the German embassy and later talked to the press. Schäfer persuaded another teen named Hartmut Hopp to smear Kneese, accusing him of sexual misconduct at the ensuing trial. Kneese then fled to Germany. As a reward, Schäfer allowed Hopp to leave the colony to study medicine because he needed a physician in the colony's hospital.

TORTURE IN A POTATO WAREHOUSE

But in 1973, a military coup brought General Pinochet to power. Schäfer supplied him with weapons. Pinochet also needed places to house the left-wing opposition to his regime, many of whom would conveniently 'disappear' (and die). Schäfer cut Pinochet a deal. Some 350 people were tortured in a potato warehouse in the colony's grounds and about 100 more were murdered and buried there.

In 1975, student activist, Erick Zott Chuecas, was arrested by the secret police and taken to the colony. He told the *Santiago Times:* 'They applied special bandages, putting wet cotton balls in my ears, putting a leather helmet over my head that covered my ears, and they tied my hands and feet. They didn't want me to know where I was being taken. When we entered the grounds of Colonia Dignidad, I had a feeling that this moment would be my last.'

His feet, legs and hands were bound and he was tied to a military camp bed. 'I was virtually immobilized,' he said. 'I was forbidden to speak and had no sense of time. They only took me out to interrogate and torture me... then, they tied me to a bed again. I would sleep from time to time and, when I woke up, I didn't know if I'd been asleep for ten minutes or two hours. Colonia Dignidad was a state within the Chilean state. It was hermetically sealed off from the outside world.'

It was so private that Pinochet and his inner circle of officers used it as a holiday destination. Nazi-hunter Simeon Wiesenthal said that Josef Mengele, the 'Angel of Death' who conducted medical experiments on inmates at Auschwitz, spent time there, while Walter Rauff, the SS *Obersturmbannführer* who invented the portable gas chamber, was known to have stayed in the area. Thus, Colonia Dignidad was known to be a stronghold of former SS officers, while the German embassy in Chile turned a blind eye.

'For many years, from the 1960s to the 1980s, German diplomats looked the other way and did too little to protect their citizens in this commune,' said German foreign minister, Frank-Walter Steinmeier. 'Even later, when Colonia Dignidad was dissolved and the people were no longer subjected to daily torture, the service lacked the determination and transparency to identify its responsibilities and to draw lessons from it.'

Pinochet stepped down as president of Chile in 1990, though he stayed on as commander-in-chief of the army until 1998. Meanwhile, activities at Colonia Dignidad came under investigation. After being charged with the sexual abuse of more than two dozen boys, Schäfer fled to Argentina where he found refuge with Hopp and his wife.

Schäfer was convicted of paedophilia in absentia. In 2006, he was arrested in Argentina and extradited back to Chile, where he was sentenced to 20 years for sexually abusing 25 children, while facing further charges which included kidnapping, forced labour, fraud and tax evasion.

He was also sentenced to three years for torture, seven years for homicide and three years for violating weapon control laws. A huge arsenal of weapons, comprising machine guns, grenades, surface-to-air missiles and Sarin nerve gas, was discovered at Colonia Dignidad. It had been stashed there by the Pinochet regime. In 2008, investigators found mass graves there. Then, they unearthed cars buried there, whose licence plates could be traced to missing political dissidents.

Schäfer died in jail in 2010 at the age of 88, just five years into his sentence. Freed from his influence, Colonia Dignidad changed its name to Villa Baviera and has become a bizarre tourist destination, which still celebrates its German heritage. Bavarian music is piped from speakers. There are restaurants, and it can be rented out as a wedding venue. Many of the former inmates continued to live there as well, too institutionalized to leave.

Meanwhile, Chile charged Hopp with aiding and abetting child abuse for bringing children to Schäfer. He and other former members of Colonia Dignidad had already been sentenced in the first instance to five years in prison. But Hopp fled to Germany and found refuge at the Free People's Mission run by the preacher, Ewald Frank, who had run guns to Schäfer and helped him set up his weapons factories. As a citizen of the German Federal Republic, Hopp could not be extradited. An investigation against him in Germany was dropped in 2019.

CHAPTER 16:

THE REICHSBÜRGER MOVEMENT

Cults tend to form around esoteric religious beliefs, but small groups of devotees can gather around any arcane idea. The *Reichsbürgerbewegung*, or Reich Citizens' Movement, for example, rejects the legitimacy of the modern Federal Republic of Germany, considering it to be a Jewish conspiracy.

Instead, members claim to be citizens of the German Reich as it existed within its pre-World War II borders in 1937. Others look back to the German Empire, or the Second Reich, following unification in 1871 – or even, the First Reich, which was the Holy Roman Empire and which lasted from 1512 to 1806. Even neo-Nazis think they're a bit extreme.

Present-day members refuse to pay federal taxes, and they issue their own passports and driving licences. Nor do they recognize the courts that seek to enforce these fiscal measures and refuse to pay the resulting fines. Many of them ascribe to right-wing populist, anti-Semitic and Nazi ideologies, and furthermore are Holocaust deniers. By 2021, while planning a putsch, they were estimated to have 21,000 members.

According to the Reichsbürgers, Nazi Germany did not

formally surrender to the Allies, and so Germany is still at war and under occupation, which is to overlook the surrender documents signed at Lüneburg Heath on 4 May 1945, Rheims on 7 May and Berlin on 8 May. Nevertheless, they maintain that the 1919 Weimar Constitution is still in effect. Although it went into abeyance under the Enabling Act of 1933, which gave the Chancellor – that is, Adolf Hitler – the power to rule without the involvement of the Reichstag, it was technically in force until the establishment of the Federal Republic of Germany (West Germany) and the German Democratic Republic (East Germany) in 1949. The current Federal Republic of Germany is merely the successor to the state of West Germany, which was forced on Germany by the Allied powers and is thus illegitimate.

SELF-MADE MEN

Reichsbürgers maintain that the German Reich is actually governed by a *Kommissarische Reichsregierung* (a provisional Reich government) or by an *Exilregierung* (a government in exile). The original *Kommissarische Reichsregierung* was set up in 1985 by Wolfgang Gerhard Günter Ebel, a disgruntled former railway employee from West Berlin, sacked for organizing a strike and a man who appointed himself Reich Chancellor. Members of his cabinet soon fell out with him and left to start their own provisional governments, including the *Exilregierung Deutsches Reich* or the *Deutsches Reich AG* (German Reich AG). Members variously proclaim themselves kings, counts, dukes, chancellors, ministers and mayors.

Under Ebel's leadership, the *Kommissarische Reichsregierung* issued building permits and other 'official' documents, along with currency and stamps for the regime. These are only recognized by the Principality of Sealand, a micro-nation set up on a sea fort built by the British in the North Sea during World War II and once occupied by a pirate radio station.

Ebel's government claims to have issued a thousand arrest warrants to those who have disregarded *Kommissarische Reichsregierung* documents, threatening to have them tried for high treason – punishable by death – if his government came to power. Later attempts to have Ebel prosecuted for impersonating a public official failed because the courts found him to be certifiably insane.

A protest by Reichsbürgers in Berlin, 2019, bearing flags of the old German Reich.

The Kingdom of Germany

There is also the *Königreich Deutschland* (kingdom of Germany), ruled by King Peter I. Former cook and karate teacher, Peter

Fitzek, was crowned in the grounds of an old hospital in Wittenberg, south-west of Berlin. Followers bought property in the village of Rutenberg where they ran seminars on how to overthrow the state for upwards of €340 (£295/$380) with promises of freedom – including from paying taxes – as well as six-hour working days, and homeopathy rather than conventional medicine. Intelligence authorities have described the offering as a 'huge scam'. The *Königreich Deutschland* has links to the Anastasia movement in Russia.

People were encouraged to part with their money in exchange for *Engelgeld* (Angelmoney) and were then unable to change it back. In 2017, Fitzek was sentenced to three years and eight months in prison for operating a bank without a licence and embezzling his clients' money, though the conviction was later quashed. However, it was not the only time Fitzek had run into trouble with the law. In 2016, he had been caught driving without a proper licence for the eighth time and claimed that he had abandoned it in favour of one he had authorized himself. He had also been previously convicted of running an illegal health insurance scheme.

Armed and dangerous

They might seem ridiculous, but the Reichsbürgers are dangerous and have been building up caches of arms for Day X – a day of reckoning when they will rise up and overthrow the German government. In 2014, a similar group calling itself the 'Free State of Prussia' attempted to build up its own militia by smuggling arms into Germany.

One Reichsbürger, Adrian Ursache – a former winner of the Mr Germany beauty pageant – violently resisted when the police tried to evict him from his property in Reuden, some 70 miles

(112 km) northwest of Berlin, after he refused to keep up loan repayments. He had declared the property as the independent mini-state of 'Ur'. A notice nailed to a tree in the garden read: 'Only the laws of the state of Ur apply. Infringements will be severely punished.' Above it was a flag in the colours of the old German Reich: black, white and red. He opened fire on the police when they raided his house in 2016. In 2019, Ursache was convicted of attempted murder and sentenced to seven years in prison. While awaiting trial, he was divorced by his wife, a former Miss Germany.

On 19 October 2016, a self-proclaimed Reichsbürger, known only as Wolfgang P., fired on a special response unit of the Bavarian police in Georgensgmünd, when they attempted to confiscate his 31 firearms after his gun licence was revoked. His letterbox bore the inscription, 'Government territory of Wolfgang' and the message: 'Here my word is law!' Three police officers were badly hurt, and one of them died later from his injuries. On 23 October 2017, Wolfgang P. was sentenced to life imprisonment.

However, the *Reichsbürgerbewegung* has even infiltrated the police itself. A Bavarian police officer was suspended from duty due to his connections with the movement, and police officers in other states are suspected of having similar connections.

One prominent member of the *Reichsbürgerbewegung* is the R&B singer Xavier Naidoo, who was born and raised in Mannheim, West Germany, to South African parents of South African Indian, Telugu, German and Irish descent. His invitation to represent Germany at the 2016 Eurovision Song Contest was withdrawn following an online petition condemning his anti-Semitic and homophobic lyrics. His 2012 song, 'Wo Sind Sie Jetzt' ('Where Are You Now') was widely criticized in Germany for implying all homosexuals were paedophiles. In another song released after the 2008 financial crisis, Naidoo referred to the banker Baron Rothschild as 'Baron Deadschild' and called him a 'schmuck', as well as blaming the Rothschild family for the worst vicissitudes of Germany's history in the 20th century.

In 2022, 25 members were arrested for allegedly planning a coup d'etat. They included the 71-year-old Heinrich XIII Prinz Reuss, who the conspirators aimed to install as the new head of state. He was supported by several former members of Germany's Special Forces Command (KSK). Eight members, including Prinz Reuss, a GP, a celebrity chef and an astrologer, went on trial for membership of a terrorist organization and for preparing an act of high treason in May 2024.

CHAPTER 17:

MOVE

Commonly known as MOVE, the Christian Movement for Life was a radical African-American group that equated satanic influence with 'the system'. It was founded in Philadelphia in 1972 by Vincent Leaphart, a high-school drop-out who could hardly read or write. However, with the help of white middle-class college lecturer Donald J. Glassey, he wrote a 300-page diatribe called *The Teachings of John Africa*, known to followers simply as 'the Book', which provided the guidelines for a militant black organization, whose symbol was a clenched fist.

Leaphart and Glassey had met on a protest march. In 1973, Leaphart established a small commune in Glassey's house in the gentrified Powelton Village area of Philadelphia. By 1975, the commune had swelled to around 35 people – both adults and children. As a protest group, they managed to disrupt a bicentennial meeting of the governors of the 13 original states of the Union (of the United States). Glassey then left the group, complaining that they advocated violence. He did not get his house back.

Noisy Neighbours

All the members of MOVE took the surname 'Africa'. The men called themselves Minister for Information and Minister of Defence. Women's role was to produce the next generation of MOVE members. Leaphart sought to control every element of his followers' lives, including childbirth. But standards at the commune were starting to slip as the place became grossly overcrowded. Huge piles of garbage became a public nuisance and neighbours complained. The police were called, but there was little they could do. MOVE's response was to build a high-security fence with loudspeakers mounted on it, so they could taunt the officers.

After being arrested for the possession of marijuana in 1978, Donald Glassey told the police that MOVE was making bombs. On the instructions of the hard-line mayor, Frank Rizzo, former

Vincent Leaphart aka John Africa.

police chief and scourge of the Black Panthers, police officers stormed the house, only to be confronted by MOVE members in combat fatigues brandishing rifles and shotguns. Others held babies and children in front of them as human shields. One policeman was killed in a shoot-out. Three others and four firemen were wounded. Nine MOVE members found themselves behind bars for life, but Leaphart had slipped out of the house before the bullets started flying.

The police caught up with him three years later in Richmond, Virginia. He stood trial on firearms charges but was acquitted. Moving into his sister's house in the Cobbs Creek area of Philadelphia, he re-established the commune. This time, he had the windows of the house boarded up and a pill-box built on the roof.

THE SIEGE

When a man armed with a shotgun appeared on the roof, the police decided it was time to act. On 8 August 1985 – the anniversary of the 1978 shoot-out – over 300 policemen and firefighters camped out around MOVE's new headquarters, starting a siege that lasted eight months. Meanwhile, members excavated a reinforced bunker in the basement. But the new African-American mayor, Wilson Goode, stayed the police's hand. In negotiations, MOVE demanded the release of all MOVE members sentenced after the 1978 siege. Something had to be done.

In the early morning of 13 May 1985, police sharpshooters took up positions sheltering behind sandbags as fire engines drove into position. Police Commissioner Gregory Sambor gave MOVE members 15 minutes to come out with their hands held up. MOVE's response was to recommend that the police check their life assurance, reminding them that one of their number had lost his life in the battle of 1978.

At 6am, the deadline up, high-pressure fire hoses were turned on the roof-top pill-box. Tear-gas grenades lobbed into the compound prompted automatic fire in response. Police started drilling through the wall of the house next door. MOVE members fired through the hole and the police fired back with machine guns.

The police broke through the wall at the other side of the house and hurled in tear-gas grenades. When officers followed, one was hit by gunfire, but his life was saved by his flak jacket. Nevertheless, the assault was called off. By this time, the police had loosed off over 10,000 rounds of ammunition.

The police decided that the thing to do was to knock the house

The aftermath of the 1985 bombing of the MOVE compound. The atrocity was one of the most shocking events in modern US history.

down. They called for a crane with a wrecking ball but could not get it down the narrow street, so the stand-off continued for the rest of the day. The families of MOVE members used bull horns to beg their loved ones to come out. That did no good either.

In the end, it was decided to bomb the building. This was unprecedented. Never before had the American civil authorities dropped a bomb on a home. At around 5.30pm, they dropped a bag full of commercial explosives from a helicopter on to the roof of the house. The idea was to dislodge the roof-top pillbox, blow a hole in the roof and pump in tear gas. But they had badly misjudged the situation.

The explosion sent wreckage flying ten metres into the air. The huge crowd that had gathered cheered, but the cheers were mixed with gasps of horror. The authorities were bombing babies, people said. When the dust cleared, the pill-box was still standing – the explosive had not been powerful enough to dislodge it.

Worse still, the explosion had set a nearby house on fire, but firefighters could not move in because MOVE members were laying down withering gunfire. A 30-year-old woman and a 13-year-old boy managed to escape under intense covering fire. They were rescued and arrested, but they were the only ones who got out alive.

By the time the fire brigade had got the blaze under control, the entire block had burned down and the fire had spread to adjoining streets. In all, nearly 60 houses were gutted. In the cellar of the MOVE headquarters, among the charred remains of children and dogs, the police eventually found what they were looking for: the body of John Africa. Eleven people were killed, including five children.

DISILLUSIONED

In September 2021, Mike and Debbie Davis and their son Mike Africa Jr spoke out for the first time about their disillusionment with MOVE. They said they had grown increasingly disturbed by the way children had been treated within the organization in the 1980s and 1990s, with some kids unable to read or write because they were kept out of school and girls as young as 12 being pressured into child marriages. They also objected to the way that MOVE members who fell sick with cancer were instructed to forgo medication on grounds that their illness was 'all in the mind'.

Mike and Debbie had served 40 years for the shooting of the police officer during the 1978 siege. Mike Jr had been born in the cell days after his mother had been arrested and was not reunited with his parents until he was 40 years old.

About three years after John Africa's death, control of the group passed to his widow, Alberta Africa, and her deputy, Sue Africa. The pair have been in charge ever since. The first defections began earlier in the summer of 2021, when 13 former members and supporters, including Mike and Debbie Davis's daughter, Whit Sims, quit. She had been forced to marry at 16 and her brother, Chuck, who had been a member of MOVE since the age of 12, had been expelled while spending 42 years behind bars for questioning the leaders' judgement.

They set up a website called Leaving MOVE, where they alleged that there had been a pattern of children as young as 12 being forced into sex, going back decades. Some married at the age of 14. A girl of 12 got pregnant. They also alleged that members were subjected to intimidation and manipulation.

Debbie and Mike Sr said that 'there were elements that fit the definition of a cult'. Mike Africa Jr went further, saying that all the classic elements of a cult were present in MOVE, including the way John Africa was revered.

'He was put on a pedestal in an unhealthy way,' he said. 'I think it was very unhealthy to praise someone so much they lose sight of themselves.'

CHAPTER 18:

NUWAUBIAN NATION

The United Nuwaubian Nation of Moors is an African-American separatist movement. Confusingly, it also known as 'Ansaru Allah Community', 'Holy Tabernacle Ministries' and 'Yamassee Native American Moors of the Creek Nation'. Its leader, charismatic black supremacist Dwight 'Malachi' York, claimed: 'We are the Indigenous people of these shores, before the settlers from Europe came to these shores spreading their way of life, their filth and religion.'

According to the *Intelligence Report of the Southern Poverty Law Center*, a periodical that monitors extremist groups in the US, Nuwaubianism 'mixes black supremacist ideas with worship of the Egyptians and their pyramids, a belief in UFOs and various conspiracies related to the Illuminati and the Bilderbergers'.

Historically, the Bavarian Illuminati were an 18th-century secret society, which sought power and influence by infiltrating the Freemasons. To modern-day conspiracy theorists, they are a shadowy brotherhood, who pull the strings in corporations and governments with the aim of establishing a New World Order. Bilderbergers are the political leaders, captains of industry and other notables who meet in an off-the-record forum every year. Again, conspiracy theorists think they are trying to rule the world.

THE SPECIAL ONE

Born in 1945, Dwight York says that, at the age of seven, he went to Egypt to learn about Islam. 'My grandfather, As Sayyid Abdur Rahman Al Mahdi, the Imaam of the Ansaars in the Sudan until AD 959, upon looking into my eyes foretold that I was the one who would possess "the light".' He continued his Islamic studies after returning to the United States.

York was arrested for statutory rape in 1964 for having sex with a 13-year-old girl. Given a suspended sentence, he was put on probation. Later that year, he was arrested for assault, possession of a deadly weapon and resisting arrest. He served three years in prison.

On his release, he became a street peddler in Harlem, selling incense and pamphlets about race, which he wrote under various pseudonyms. He picked up a handful of followers and founded a sect he called Ansar Pure Sufi in keeping with the black nationalists' embrace of Islam. However, his teachings soon began to deviate from the Koran.

Dwight 'Malachi' York.

In the early 1970s, the sect moved to Brooklyn, where it became known as the Ansaru Allah Community. They supported themselves by selling pamphlets, and people were encouraged to come and hear the preaching of the self-styled Dr Malachi Z. York, though he changed his name a number of times, calling himself variously 'The Supreme Grand Master Dr. Malachi Z. York', 'Nayya Malachizodoq-El' and 'Issa al Haadi al Mahdi'. Soon, the Ansaru Allah Community were running bookshops, gift shops, clothes shops and grocery shops. Branches of the church opened in Trinidad, London and Toronto. York also dabbled in the music business in an attempt to reach a wider audience.

HARSH CONDITIONS

Five hundred Ansaru Allah Community members lived in 20 barracks-style apartments in the Bushwick district of Brooklyn. In order to join the cult, recruits were required to surrender their possessions and work for free. Those who did not sell their quota of pamphlets were beaten. Members had to ask permission to have sex, even with their spouses, and York used female members – some of whom were underage – as his personal harem.

As its popularity increased, the Ansaru Allah Community had enough money to move to a mansion in the Catskills worth $5 million (£3.9m). It was here that York molested girls as young as six and had sex with 12-year-olds. Meanwhile, the offshoots of the sect proliferated – 'Holy Tabernacle Ministries', 'Egiptian [*sic*] Church of Karast,' 'Holy Seed Baptist Synagogue', 'Ancient Mystic Order of Melchizedek', 'Ancient Egiptian [*sic*] Order', 'All Eyez on Egypt', 'United Nuwaubian Nation of Moors', 'Yamassee Native American Tribe', 'Washitaw Tribe' and 'Lodge 19 of the Ancient and Mystic Order of Malachizodok'.

With their own print shop, they began producing books, often plagiarizing other New Age works. They mixed together stories about UFOs, the religion of ancient Egypt, the myth of Atlantis and Bible stories. Borrowing from the Nation of Islam, York claimed that white people were 'devils', whose light skin was the result of leprosy and having sex with dogs. He himself was an extraterrestrial master teacher from the planet Rizq, who had been visiting Earth before humans evolved, arriving in his current avatar by spaceship in 1945 or turning up in 1970 on the Comet Bennett.

In 1993, the cult moved to a remote 476-acre estate in Putnam County, Georgia. This may have been prompted by an FBI investigation into offences allegedly committed by members, including arson, welfare fraud, extortion and the illegal possession of weapons. In Georgia, York abandoned Islam and claimed to be a Native American, calling himself 'Chief Black Eagle' of the 'Yamassee Tribe of Native Americans'. He also claimed to be, simultaneously, a god from outer space, a member of the Sudanese royal family and a descendant of the Olmec people of Mesoamerica – where polygamy and underage sex were part of the culture, apparently.

Adopting an ancient Egyptian motif, the cult then became known as the 'United Nuwaubian Nation of Moors'. They built two wood-and-plaster pyramids in their compound, 'Tama-Re' or 'Kodesh' or 'Wahannee' or 'The Golden City' or 'Al Tamaha'. To make money, York set up a nightclub called Club Ramses in one of the pyramids. When the police closed it down for violating zoning regulations, the county sheriff received death threats. The attorney representing the county against the Nuwaubians was harassed and the county government disrupted. York claimed the closure of the club was racist, and Al Sharpton and Jesse Jackson came along to lend their support.

York's oldest son, Jacob, who had left the cult in 1990, confronted his father for his blatant charlatanism. York shamelessly retorted: 'I don't believe in any of this shit. If I had to dress up like a nun, if I had to be a Jew, I'd do it for this type of money.'

THE RAID

The authorities had realized something was wrong when a number of underage Nuwaubian girls had given birth in local hospitals. Fearing a Waco-style shoot-out, the FBI waited until York Senior left the compound before arresting him. Then, on 8 May 2002, 300 agents raided the compound, where they met no resistance.

York was indicted on 120 counts, including 74 counts of child molestation, 29 counts of aggravated child molestation and one count of rape. Five charges of racketeering and six of transporting children across state lines for the purpose of sex followed.

Accepting a plea bargain, York faced just 15 years in jail. But a federal judge threw this out, and York got 135 years. The federal government seized Tama-Re and York's assets and evicted his followers. Many kept the faith, though, turning out at the hearings where his appeals have been consistently rejected. As things stand, he won't be eligible for parole until 2122.

The cult continues its activities to this day in Brooklyn under the umbrella 'United Sabaeans World', who have a global chain of bookshops. Their website claims that 'The Master Teacher Dr. Malachi Z. K. York' is detained illegally. Followers still believe in their extraterrestrial origins.

HERMETIC CULTS

Hermetic cults claim to have secret knowledge that is only revealed to members, but usually only a discrete inner circle, which your average Joe might join if they are able to devote the whole of their life and most of their money to climbing up the greasy pole. Sometimes, this embraces devil worship, which involves more than stripping off your kit and dancing around the woods at night. That might be a good deal more fun than what hardcore Satanists get up to, which can even involve murder. Or so they claim. Like all the cults in this book, they are best avoided.

CHAPTER 19:

ORDO TEMPLI ORIENTIS

The Ordo Templi Orientis – or 'Order of the Temple of the East' or 'Order of Oriental Templars' – was basically a secretive spin-off from Freemasonry in the German-speaking world. However, when it came to England, it was hijacked by the occultist Aleister Crowley, once dubbed 'the wickedest man in the world'.

Crowley was born in 1875 to a family of Plymouth Brethren. Early on, he rebelled. He took to drink and drugs, slept with his mother's maidservant and asked for the body of his still-born sister to experiment on. When this was refused, he went to work on a live cat, testing out whether it really did have nine lives. He dosed it with arsenic, chloroformed it, hung it over a gas jet, stabbed it, drowned it, cut its throat, smashed its skull, burned it and threw it from an upstairs window. The cat did not survive. It was Crowley's own mother who first called him The Beast – after the Great Beast in the Book of Revelation – a name he readily accepted.

At Trinity College, Cambridge, Crowley changed his name from Edward Alexander to Aleister and began his lifelong study of the occult. Age 23, he joined the Hermetic Order of the Golden Dawn, a secret society set up by Freemasons who were also Rosicrucians – that is, members of the *Societas Rosicruciana in Anglia*, an esoteric Christian order.

To practise the magic he learned there, Crowley rented Boleskin House on Loch Ness, where he tried to conjure up his guardian angel. Legend has it that he summoned up a host of evil spirits instead.

Aleister Crowley.

BIZARRE BEHAVIOUR

Crowley's bizarre and disruptive behaviour resulted in both his and his mentor Samuel Liddell Mathers' expulsion from the Order. He soon fell out with Mathers over sex. A professed celibate, Mathers insisted on six months' abstinence by his followers. Crowley could not manage this and initiated a magical ceremony that involved the deflowering of young girls. This resulted in the prosecution of two cult members for rape.

In 1903, he met and married the psychic medium, Rose Kelly. Honeymooning in Cairo in 1904, Crowley supposedly conjured up a spirit called Aiwass. Speaking through Rose, Aiwass dictated Crowley's most famous book, *Liber Al vel Legis* or *The Book of the Law*. It said that Christianity was about to be swept away and replaced by a new religious order. Its Messiah would be Crowley, of course, and he proclaimed himself: 'The Great Beast 666, Prophet of the New Aeon'. Rose became his first Scarlet Woman, after the biblical consort of the Beast.

Aiwass encouraged Crowley to take all the drugs he could lay his hands on. The message for the New Age was simple. Satan was not an external force. He was found within the heart of every man and woman; he was the source of unlimited power which could be released simply by discarding all moral scruples.

In 1905, Crowley went on an expedition to the Himalayas. Climbing the world's third-highest mountain, Kangchenjunga, six of the party fell. Crowley refused to go and rescue them. Four died. He also treated the porters brutally, making them walk barefoot on ice grounds. There were persistent rumours that he had eaten one or two. In the end, he abandoned the expedition and absconded with the money.

'Do what thou wilt shall be the whole of the law,' wrote Crowley. This was not an original thought. It had been the motto of the co-educational Abbey of Thélème in the first book of François Rabelais' satirical classic, *The History of Gargantua and Pantagruel*, published in 1532.

BROKEN WOMEN

In 1907, Crowley set up his own cult, *Argentum Astrum*, the Order of the Silver Star. On a mountain-top in Morocco in 1909 with his acolyte Victor Neuburg, Crowley had a revelation that sex was linked to magic. He took Australian violinist, Leila Waddell, as his second Scarlet Woman, or 'Divine Whore', who had 'the mark of the Beast' tattooed between her breasts. By then, Rose was drinking a bottle of whisky a day. Divorced, Rose was committed to a lunatic asylum two years later. His second wife, Nicaraguan beauty, Maria de Miramar, suffered the same fate and a number of his other Scarlet Women were institutionalized, committed suicide or drank themselves to death after parting from Crowley.

Even when he was middle-aged, bald and bloated, he continued to attract women. Having filed his teeth to sharp points, he simply sank them into the wrists of women he fancied. In 1934, a 19-year-old girl threw herself at him in the street and insisted that he give her a baby. After he bedded her, she ended up in an asylum too.

Leila Waddell.

He did not confine his sexual interests to women. Poet Victor Neuburg became the centrepiece of Crowley's occult ceremonies, which usually involved sodomy within a pentagram inside a circle. In Paris, Crowley and Neuburg conducted a series of rituals, where Neuburg had his buttocks scourged and an inverted cross was carved on his chest, then he was ritually sodomized. Blood was drunk and faeces eaten. Snakes were released and a frog was baptized 'Jesus of Nazareth', then crucified.

In 1912, a German Freemason, Theodor Reuss, visited Crowley in Scotland. He was head of the secretive Ordo Templi Orientis, which had been founded in Germany in 1904. It claimed to possess the key to all Masonic and hermetic secrets, which were revealed bit by bit as you rose through the nine grades of the cult. Although rituals involved a dagger and a chalice to represent symbolic sexual intercourse, there was also a more hands-on approach to sexual magic.

Reuss accused Crowley of stealing OTO's secret rituals. But Crowley managed to convince Reuss that he had stumbled on the rituals by his own devices and Reuss invited Crowley to join. Within five years, Crowley had completely taken over OTO, which then became a vehicle for Crowley's Satanism.

'My master is Satan,' said Crowley. 'Resist not evil.'

To escape the interest of the press and debts he had run up through his addiction to cocaine and heroin, Crowley moved to a derelict farmhouse near Cefalu in northern Sicily. There, he set up home with Leah Hirsig, a school mistress he had met in New York in 1918, who could match his staggering drug consumption. Her friend, Ninette Shumway, acted as nanny for their short-lived daughter, Toupée. Crowley also called Shumway his Second Concubine.

BLACK MASS

They converted the farmhouse into a satanic temple and called it the Abbey of Thelema, where he kept bloodstained neckties he said had belonged to Jack the Ripper. The floor of the central hall had a circle and a pentagram painted inside it. The walls were hung with obscene and blasphemous paintings. One showed Knight Templars' goat-devil Baphomet – a name that Crowley had taken for himself – sodomizing a man. A whip, a phallus and a copy of Crowley's *Black Book of Rituals* lay on the altar. Devotees would celebrate Black Mass there. Crowley would eat a communion wafer smeared with Leah Hirsig's excrement. He would disembowel a live cat, collect its blood and drink it. In one ceremony, Leah had sex with a goat, whose throat was cut at the climax of the ritual. The blood was collected and consumed.

One visitor, the American actress, Jane Wolfe, found the farmhouse – or perhaps Crowley's domestic arrangements – so squalid that she lived in a tent outside for three years, practising yoga nude on the beach. The artist's model, Betty May, was also appalled, but her husband, Raoul Loveday, was seduced. He collapsed and died after drinking the blood of a sacrificial cat.

Back in London, May spoke to the *Sunday Express* and newspapers had a field day with lurid tales of drugs, magic and 'vile practices'.

Then, when a child went missing from a nearby village, Crowley was accused of kidnapping and killing it. No charges were brought, but Italy's dictator Benito Mussolini ordered Crowley's expulsion and locals whitewashed over Crowley's murals.

Leah followed Crowley into exile. She tolerated his new mistresses, but, in 1925, he took another woman named Dorothy Olsen as his new Scarlet Woman. Leah stayed on as his secretary, though her sister published an exposé in the *New York*

Journal. But gradually sanity prevailed. In 1930, Leah returned to America and went back to schoolteaching.

Crowley wrote his autobiography Confessions, which was published posthumously, an autobiographical novel called *The Diary of a Drug Fiend* and a number of pornographic works. He also painted, exhibiting his work in 1930 in Berlin where he met Aldous Huxley and Alfred Adler. Supported by OTO members in Germany, he produced *Magick in Theory and Practice*, spelling magic with an added 'k' to distinguish his occult magic from conjuring.

Crowley also wrote a commentary on *The Book of the Law*, which emphasizes the importance of animals and possibly human sacrifice. He concludes: 'A male child of perfect innocence and high intelligence is the most satisfactory and suitable victim.'

HUMAN SACRIFICE

In a footnote, Crowley claimed to have performed such human sacrifices on an average of 150 times a year between 1912 and 1928 – killing over 2,000 children. And he was unrepentant. In a court case in 1934, Crowley was asked:

'Do you believe as a magician in bloody sacrifice?'

He replied: 'Yes.'

'You say for nearly all purposes human sacrifice is best?'

'Yes, it is,' he said.

Crowley's *Magick in Theory and Practice* remains the bible of modern Satanists. After its publication, Crowley subsided into poverty, hastened by his heroin and cocaine addiction. He spent his twilight years in a private hotel called Netherwood in Hastings. He died in Brighton in 1947 at the age of 72. His body was cremated in a Black Mass and his ashes were sent to his successor, Karl Germer.

Germer had been arrested and interned by the Nazis in 1935 because of his association with Crowley. In 1941, with the help of his American wife, he was deported to the US where he set up a number of new lodges in California. One of them was the Church of Thelema in Hollywood. It was run by Jack Parsons, who was a rocket scientist and had developed jet-assisted take-off during World War II. Earlier, Parsons had been a disciple of Wilfred Smith, who had held devil-worshipping parties at Agape Lodge in the 1930s, attracting the Hollywood crowd.

In 1946, Parsons attempted to bring the 'Whore of Babylon' down from the astral plane and make her incarnate in the womb of a woman. While chanting various incantations, Parsons had sex repeatedly with a willing devotee, while another OTO member, science-fiction writer L. Ron Hubbard, made copious notes. When Crowley heard about this bizarre experiment, he wrote it off as 'idiotic'. Indeed, the woman did not even get pregnant. The experiment left Parsons exhausted. Hubbard ran off with Parsons' girlfriend and $10,000 (£7,500) of his money and started the Church of Scientology.

Distraught, Parsons changed his name to Belarion Armillus Al Dajjal, the Antichrist 'who am come to fulfil the law of the Beast 666'. In 1952, he blew himself up in a chemical explosion in the basement laboratory of his home. Hubbard later claimed to have studied under Crowley.

CHAPTER 20:

SCIENTOLOGY

At its peak, the Church of Scientology claimed to have eight million members worldwide, which meant that it was far and away the biggest of the non-Christian cults. It is also one of the wealthiest, most secretive and most litigious.

It was the brainchild of prolific science fiction writer, L. Ron Hubbard, who incorporated the Church of Scientology in New Jersey in 1953. The Church of Scientology of California, which became the cult's headquarters, was incorporated in Los Angeles in 1954. Then, it began its march towards world domination in 1959, opening a branch at Saint Hill Manor, near East Grinstead in Sussex, England.

Hubbard was born in 1911 in Tilden, Nebraska. His father was an officer in the US Navy. A promising student at school, Hubbard went to George Washington University, where he studied civil engineering but left after one term and began writing pulp fiction.

During World War II, he served in the US Navy. He had two commands but was removed from each one. He never saw action and was invalided out with a duodenal ulcer.

During the 1940s, Hubbard was a friend of the writer A. E. van Vogt, who created the fictional 'Science of Nexialism' – an advanced and beneficial form of psychological conditioning.

Hubbard came up with his own version, which appeared in a 40-page article in the magazine *Astounding Science Fiction* in April 1950. It was so well received that Hubbard dashed out the classic, *Dianetics: The Modern Science of Mental Health*. Aping Sigmund Freud, Hubbard said the unconscious or 'reactive' mind stores the trauma of every unpleasant thing that has ever happened, even though the conscious mind has forgotten them. These unconscious memories or 'engrams' begin to be stored even before we are born.

The aim of Dianetics is to rid the individual of all their engrams and make them a 'Clear'. This is done by a technique called 'auditing', whereby the auditor takes the 'Pre-Clear' individual back to the source of the engram. In other words, it is a form of psychotherapy. Scientologists believe that engrams can simply be removed by this form of counselling or confession. But, of course, this takes several hundred hours of auditing, which costs thousands of pounds. Then, there are all the engrams you have accumulated in past lives to deal with. Nevertheless, once you are Clear you stay Clear. This gives you total recall and you can make mathematical calculations or solve chess problems that would normally have taken hours in a matter of seconds.

Dianetics was poorly received by the scientific and medical press. *Scientific American* said that Hubbard's book contained 'more promises and less evidence per page than any publication since the invention of printing', while *The New Republic* called it a 'bold and immodest mixture of complete nonsense and perfectly reasonable common sense, taken from long acknowledged findings and disguised and distorted by a crazy, newly invented terminology'. Fellow science-fiction writers weren't convinced either. Isaac Asimov considered it 'gibberish', while Jack Williamson called it 'a lunatic revision of Freudian psychology'.

L. Ron Hubbard in 1950.

RUNAWAY SUCCESS

Nevertheless, the public in therapy-crazed America lapped it up and *Dianetics* quickly became a best-seller. Dianetics groups sprang up all over the country. Hubbard himself set up the Hubbard Dianetic Research Foundation, but it rapidly ran out of money. In 1952, it went bankrupt and Hubbard sold out his interest, which included his copyright in Dianetics: *The Modern Science of Mental Health*, to one of his backers, Don Purcell.

Hubbard then set up the Association of Scientologists and sued Purcell for the use of his ideas. Purcell eventually gave the rights back and went to work on a similar idea called synergetics. Then, Scientology became a church, even though its adherents deny that it is a religion. Hubbard was frank about the move.

'You don't get rich writing science fiction. If you want to get rich, you start a religion.'

Back in the 1940s, when Hubbard had been discussing writers' perennial money problems with other authors, he quoted George Orwell, who said he'd always thought there might be a lot of cash in starting a new religion. In 1955, the Church of Scientology was awarded tax-exempt status as a non-profit-making organization. But within three years, the US Internal Revenue Service were attempting to withdraw that status.

The next 'breakthrough' was the development of the E-meter. Like a primitive lie detector, an E-meter measures skin conductivity. It is said to detect the presence of engrams, indicating whether the subject is Clear or not. The bog-standard 1995 version costs $625 (£485), though the latest Mark Super VII model costs a whacking $3,850 (£3,000). However, by the Church of Scientology's own admission, it does not work.

In 1963, America's Food and Drug Administration raided the Church of Scientology in Washington and seized all the E-meters on the grounds that it is illegal in the US to practise any form of medical diagnosis or therapy without medical qualifications. A 1969 court ruling allowed Scientologists to use E-meters only on the assumption that they were totally ineffective. That did not stop them from being a money-spinner.

GOING CLEAR

When it came to being a money-making machine, there was an intrinsic problem with early Scientology. Once you became Clear, where do you go from there? To maintain the structure of a cult, there must be inner groups and further ladders to climb until the Clear crosses, as Scientology puts it, 'the bridge to total freedom'.

There are now eight levels, each costing $1,000. Of course, the details have to be kept secret. This is because if you are not properly prepared by each succeeding stage, the knowledge revealed could be dangerous to you.

Level Three, known as 'The Wall of Fire', for example, nearly killed L. Ron Hubbard when he discovered it, he claimed, so if you don't have your life assurance payments up to date, look away now.

Level Three teaches that, 75 million years ago, the galaxy was overpopulated. The dictator Xenu persuaded billions of beings from the 75 inhabited planets in the Galactic Federation to go to Teegeeack or the planet we call Earth. He chained them up in the volcanoes on Hawaii and bombarded them with nuclear bombs. This released their inner selves, or Theta beings, from their bodies. The disembodied Theta beings, or Thetans, were transported to the Canary Islands, where they were frozen in alcohol, wrapped up tight and blasted out across the solar system. This whole process was pretty traumatic, so these inter-planetary daiquiris are chock full of engrams. Naturally, they want to have bodies again. Millions of them cluster around every one of us, bringing with them their engrams, which are responsible for sexual perversion, religion and all the other troubles in the world. That's why you have to start the auditing process all over again to clear engrams that are not even yours.

Now that didn't hurt, did it? If you survived, read on.

Not surprisingly, clearing these 'Body Thetans' is a long and costly business. Well, you didn't think it was going to be cheap, did you? The auditor must take the initiate back 75 million years to clear the cause of the problem.

TAXING QUESTIONS

Governments around the world soon began having problems with the Church of Scientology, especially over its claims for tax-exempt status as a religious organization while claiming not to be religious at all. In 1965, the Australian government set up a Board of Inquiry, which stands as the most thorough-going investigation into the cult. Its report concluded: 'Scientology is evil, its techniques evil, its practice a serious threat to the community, medically, morally and socially, and its adherents sadly deluded and often mentally ill.'

Furthermore, Scientology 'is a delusional belief system, based on fiction and fallacies and propagated by falsehood and deception'. And the Board of Inquiry dismissed the cult as 'the world's largest organization of unqualified persons engaged in the practice of dangerous techniques which masquerade as mental therapy'.

Consequently, Scientology was banned in Australia until 1983. The following year, it was given tax-exempt status as a religion.

In 1968, Britain banned foreign Scientologists from coming to the UK to study or work. That ban was lifted in 1980. But in a British court case in 1984, the judge came to much the same conclusion as the Australian Board of Inquiry.

'Scientology is both immoral and socially obnoxious,' he said. 'In my judgement, it is corrupt, sinister and dangerous. It is based on lies and deceit and has as its real objective [creating] money and power for Mr Hubbard, his wife and those close to him at the top.'

Scientology may have made L. Ron Hubbard very rich but, on a personal level, things were not going too smoothly for him. In 1959, his oldest son, Ron Junior, declared publicly that his father was insane. The child of Hubbard's second marriage, his daughter Alexis, Hubbard said, had in fact been fathered by Jack Parsons – so maybe Parsons' experiment did work after all.

In 1966, Hubbard quit as head of the Church of Scientology, though he kept all his financial interests in it intact. He started the maritime wing of Scientology, Sea Org, and went back to sea. He spent the rest of his life sailing around the world, conveniently offshore for tax purposes. His three sea-going vessels were crewed by an elite band of Scientologists called

Messengers, who were largely teenage girls. No surprise there then. They did everything for him and were subjected to stringent punishment for even the most minor infraction.

SILENCING THE CRITICS

On shore, discipline was similarly draconian. Auditing had to be done in precisely the way that Hubbard had specified. Not even the slightest deviation was permitted. One former Scientologist claimed adherents were expected to exhibit the mentality of soldier ants. In 1966, Hubbard declared that critics of Scientology should be investigated and undermined. Any tactic was fair game against their opponents who might be 'tricked, sued or lied to or destroyed'. Dirty tricks were used to blacken the name of individuals who opposed them.

The Church set up an intelligence unit called the Guardian's Office, now known as the Office of Special Affairs, to infiltrate organizations who were deemed threatening. In Operation Freakout, it harassed author, Paulette Cooper, who had published *The Scandal of Scientology* in 1971. The plan aimed to have Cooper imprisoned or committed to a psychiatric hospital. Then, the FBI discovered evidence that there was a plot against Cooper, leading the Church to make an out-of-court settlement.

The FBI also uncovered Operation Snow White, which aimed to purge unfavourable records about Scientology and L. Ron Hubbard. This project included wiretapping and a series of infiltrations into and thefts from 136 government agencies, foreign embassies and consulates as well as private organizations critical of Scientology, carried out by Church members in more than 30 countries.

The top target was the Internal Revenue Service. In the early 1970s, cult members discovered that the tax authorities were launching a major investigation into the Church. In a covert operation, they stole hundreds of documents from the IRS offices in Los Angeles. The US government responded by sending in the FBI. Nine senior Scientologists, including Hubbard's third wife, Mary Sue, were arrested. She eventually served a year in prison after a number of appeals failed.

Hubbard suffered another personal tragedy when his second son, Quentin, committed suicide. He was gay and the Church condemned homosexuality. In 1978, Hubbard was convicted of fraud in Paris and sentenced *in absentia* to four years in prison. In the late 1970s, Hubbard had a series of heart attacks and a young acolyte named David Miscavige began taking over the organization, expelling all those who stood in his way. By 1982, he was in full control.

By this time, Hubbard was living such a reclusive life that few people know for certain when he died. Some say it was as early as 1983, though his demise was not announced until January 1986.

Since Miscavige took over, there have been FBI investigations into suspected human trafficking and slavery within the Church. Disaffected members and those forced out by Miscavige's putsch claim that his rule is rigid and authoritarian – though when they say so in print, they are slapped with a writ.

There have also been civil suits alleging kidnapping, stalking, libel, slander, invasion of privacy, harassment, rape and the sexual assault of children by senior Scientologists. Nevertheless, Scientology still boasts celebrity adherents such as Tom Cruise and John Travolta. It seems if you have enough money and are willing to believe the unbelievable unquestioningly, then you are welcome to join.

CHAPTER 21:

THE CHURCH OF SATAN

The Christian idea of Satan begins in Jewish tradition. Indeed, the word 'satan' comes from Hebrew. It means an opponent or enemy, so there are numerous 'satans'. Only in the Book of Job is Satan a single character. It opens with a curious courtroom scene where the Satan, or the accuser, challenges God's way of rewarding righteous people like Job. The Satan says that Job is only acting righteous because of God's generous provision. But if God were to let him truly suffer, then Job's true character would emerge. It doesn't. Though puzzled, Job emerges faithful.

Things changed when the Jews lived in exile among the Babylonians, who had a pantheon of evil spirits. The Children of Israel also seem to have picked up on the Greeks' child-god Astaroth, the Persian Asmodeus and the Zoroastrian Prince of Evil, Ahriman. Other religions have their lords of the underworld and personifications of evil.

By the time the New Testament was written, Satan had become established as a figure in his own right. The Gospel According to St Matthew refers to him as the 'Prince of Demons'. In his letter to the Ephesians, St Paul writes of Satan tempting the good into wickedness.

In the Christian mind, the Devil seems to have become personified in the image of the Greek god Dionysus, who was a horned god, half-man, half-goat. This horned goat appears again in the persecution of the Knights Templar and the Cathars.

Worship of the goat-creature made another appearance in a trial in Toulouse in 1335, when 63 men and women were tried for witchcraft and sorcery. One of the defendants, Catherine Delort, admitted to killing two of her aunts and said that, at the cult's Sabbats, children were killed and eaten. Another of the accused defended these actions by saying that, although God was king of the heavens, Satan was master of the world.

The Sabbats, or ceremonies, took place on high, flat ground with a wood or grove at one end. An effigy of Satan – the goat-like creature with a human body, horns and erect penis – stood on a stone altar. The worshippers carried torches lit from a flame that burned between the horns of the idol. The priestess was a young girl who prayed to the Lord Satan, then she kissed the idol. In some accounts, she kissed it on the rump, in others on the erect phallus.

A medieval image of Satan.

Hallucinogenic herbs mixed with alcohol were then taken and the priestess would lie naked across the altar. A male worshipper would then play the part of the Devil, reciting a version of the Christian creed with the name Satan substituted for Christ. The priestess was sacrificed and her body was mutilated and burned. An orgy would follow, often involving children and generally employing sodomy rather than vaginal intercourse.

Some of these ceremonies were presided over by rogue priests. In the Black Mass, water replaced the wine and black turnip was substituted for bread, while urine was sprinkled over the congregation instead of holy water. Sometimes children were sacrificed.

RITUAL MAGIC

The French knight, Gilles de Rais, followed in this tradition. Born in 1405, he was the bodyguard and companion in arms of Joan of Arc. When she was burned to death – a punishment in which de Rais took great pleasure, some say – he retired to his estates in Brittany. There, he squandered his fortune on art and a lavish court. When his family obtained a decree from the King of France to prevent him from selling off or mortgaging any more of his inheritance, he turned to alchemy and the occult. He gathered around him a group of Satanists and started practising ritual magic in the cellars of his château at Tiffauges.

His servants were sent out to procure children – usually boys between six and 12. The children were tortured and sexually abused. Then, they were killed, often at the point of orgasm. Once dead, they would be sexually abused again. De Rais took particular delight in mutilating their bodies, which were then ritually burnt. When he was arrested, he confessed, under threat of torture, that he and his followers murdered over 800 children in the name of Satan.

In 1633, French priest Urbain Grandier, a well-known womanizer and deflowerer of virgins, was accused of sending the Asmodeus, the demon of lust, to commit evil and impious acts with the nuns from the local Ursuline convent. The Mother Superior accused Grandier of using black magic to seduce her, as did other nuns. His home was searched and a diabolical pact he had signed with a number of demons was found. It was written backwards in Latin and signed in Grandier's own blood, though it is not clear whether this was a forgery or if Grandier had signed it under duress. He was tortured but refused to confess. Nevertheless, he was burned alive at the stake.

Ten years later, there was an outbreak of Satanism at the Monastère de Saint-Louise de Louvier in Paris. Father Pierre David, the confessor there, encouraged the nuns to go about their devotions naked, arguing that the nudity of Adam and Eve showed their innocence. They took communion stripped to the waist and practised lesbianism in the chapel. When Father David died, his place was taken by Father Mathurin Picard, who pursued a young nun named Sister Madeleine Bavent, gave her magic potions and made her pregnant.

When Picard died, Father Thomas Boulle took over. Bavent claimed that the two men had abducted her and taken her to a witches' Sabbat. There, she was married to the Devil, whom she called 'Dagon', committed sexual acts with him on the altar and alleged that two men were crucified and disembowelled as these acts took place. Other nuns also reported they had been brought to secret Sabbats by Picard and Boulle, where sexual intercourse with demons, particularly Dagon, took place.

Father Boulle was burned alive. The corpse of Father Picard was exhumed and burned, while Sister Bavent was imprisoned for life in the church dungeon.

THE AGE OF ARSENIC

Another satanic cult was discovered in Paris in 1673. The investigation began when two priests told the Paris police commissioner, Nicolas de la Reynie, that they had heard a string of disturbing confessions from wealthy men and women. A number of them admitted to murdering their respective husbands and wives. The priests would not break the sanctity of the confessional and give their names, but de la Reynie decided to investigate the matter.

The middle of the 17th century was known in France as the Age of Arsenic. The poison was widely available as it was used in the facial cosmetics that were all the rage. It was hard to detect and the symptoms of arsenic poisoning are much like those of cholera. Evidence of arsenic poisoning was not successfully used in court until 1840. As the chances of getting caught were limited, murder using arsenic became positively fashionable, especially among the upper classes.

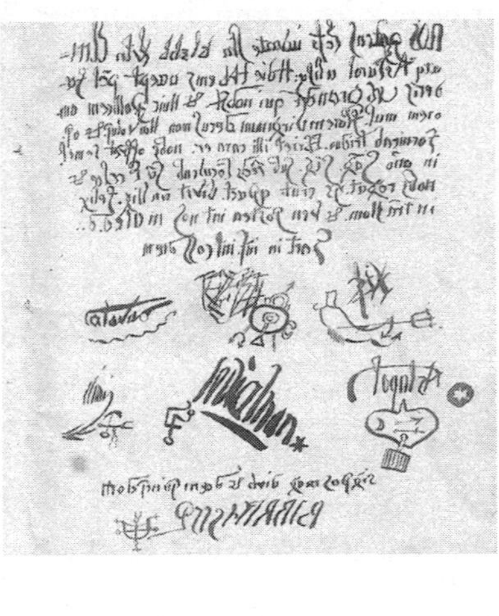

The pact between Grandier and the devil presented at his trial.

At first, de la Reynie thought he was after a gang of crooks who were selling the aristocracy 'inheritance powders'. They were so called since they were often used to dispose of an unwanted spouse or relative to secure the succession of the poisoner to the victim's property and titles.

Suspicion fell on a fortune-teller named Marie Bosse. De la Reynie sent an undercover agent to consult the clairvoyant on the best way to get rid of her troublesome husband. Madame Bosse sold her some arsenic and was arrested, along with her husband, her two sons and another fortune-teller named La Vigourex, who admitted to sleeping with all the members of the Bosse family. A huge cache of poison was found in the Bosses' home. Facing torture, La Vigourex and the Bosse family provided a list of their clients. These included prominent members of Louis XIV's court.

Plainly, this was a very delicate matter politically, but de la Reynie explained that, although an investigation might embarrass important courtiers, an epidemic of poisoning was going on. Fearing that he might find himself the next victim, Louis set up a commission of inquiry.

Officially known as *La Commission de l'Arsenic*, it was known to those who appeared before it as *L'Affaire de la Chambre Ardente* because de la Reynie, with theatrical flair, conducted the investigation in a room draped in black and lit solely by candlelight. In *La Chambre Ardente* ('the fiery chamber'), Marie Bosse and La Vigourex admitted they were part of a devil-worship cult headed by one La Voisin – real name Catherine Deshayes.

Madame Deshayes was the wife of a failed haberdasher, who had set up in business making skin-cleansing treatments, giving her access to a lot of arsenic.

As a sideline, Madame Deshayes worked as an astrologer. To lend weight to her predictions, she developed a network of informants, who, like La Voisin and La Vigourex, took pseudonyms. With an eye for a potential client, La Voisin would predict that a woman's unwanted husband, say, was going to die suddenly. If the woman appeared pleased at the prospect, La Voisin would then sell her some poison to hasten the event.

The business was so lucrative that La Voisin could afford to pay 30,000 *livres* for a secluded house in a rundown area of Paris. It was protected by a high wall and hidden by trees. Madame Deshayes lived there with her husband, now a successful jeweller, her 21-year-old daughter, Marie-Marguerite Montvoisin, and their lodger, Nicholas Levasseur – an executioner by trade.

De la Reynie put the house under surveillance. One of his agents, working undercover, overheard one of Deshayes' assistants in a bar drunkenly describing acts of devil worship. The police then picked up two people, who had attended meetings at Deshayes' house.

SATANIC RITUALS

Under interrogation, they said that Deshayes and the 66-year-old L'Abbé Etienne Guibourg regularly conducted Black Masses there. During the service, a naked woman would act as an altar table. The Abbé, wearing a chasuble embroidered with black phalluses, would rest the chalice and wafers stolen from a local church on her stomach. Intoning words from the Catholic mass, with the words 'infernal lord Satan' substituted for 'God' and 'Christ', the wafer would be pressed against the breasts and vulva of the woman. A child would urinate in the chalice and the contents would be sprinkled over the worshippers. Then, the wafer was inserted into the woman's vagina, while the Abbé chanted: 'Lord Satan sayeth "in rioting and drunkenness I rise again. You shall fulfil the lusts of the flesh. The works of the flesh are manifest – they are drunkenness, revelling, immodesty, fornication, luxury and witchcraft. My flesh is meat indeed."'

An orgy followed.

The police raided Deshayes' house. In a pavilion in the garden, they found a room draped in black with an altar in it. The candles on the altar were made from fat distilled from human flesh.

Under interrogation, Deshayes' daughter, Marie-Marguerite, told the police that animals had been sacrificed and their blood drunk. Then, she admitted that there had been human sacrifices, too.

During the ceremony, she said, the Abbé had intoned: 'Astaroth, Asmodeus, prince of friendship, I beg you to accept the sacrifice of this child, which we now offer you.'

Then, Guibourg held an infant up by its feet and slit its throat. The blood spurted into the chalice on the belly of the naked woman. The Abbé then smeared the blood on his penis and the vagina of the woman and had sex with her.

One of the children used in these sacrifices had been Deshayes'

LA MESSE NOIRE DE L'ABBÉ GUIBOURG (FIN DU XVIIe SIÈCLE)
(Enfant égorgé; l'autel c'est la Montespan

A Black Mass conducted by Etienne Guibourg, involving a child sacrifice.

own goddaughter, Françoise Filastre. Others had been supplied by the inner circle of devotees and a compliant midwife. Madame Deshayes had another sideline, as an abortionist, and often supplied living foetuses ripped from her unsuspecting clients. Victims' entrails were distilled for occult use and the rest of their bodies were burned in a stove.

It turned out that one of the worshippers was none other than Françoise-Athénaïs de Rochechouart de Mortemart, Marquise of Montespan, who had been the king's mistress for 12 years. Fearing that she was losing the king's favour to a younger lover, the Duchesse de Fontages, she attended three of the 'love masses' to try and win back his favour by acting as the nude altar table. Consequently, much of the evidence had to be hushed up.

Nevertheless, Catherine Deshayes and the Abbé Guibourg were arrested. They confessed to murdering hundreds of children over a career in Satanism that spanned 13 years. Some 150 courtiers were arrested for poisoning and sentenced to death, slavery in the French galleys or banishment. Madame Deshayes herself was burned at the stake in 1680. However, Marquise de Montespan returned, briefly, to favour.

THE DARK ARTS IN BRITAIN

There were sporadic reports of similar practices in Britain. In 1541, the English parliament outlawed witchcraft and Satanism. In 1562, they became capital offences. And in 1563, 'witchcraft, sorcery and necromancy' were also outlawed in Scotland.

The 17th century saw the rise of the witchfinder and over 30,000 people were put to death for devil worship. Nevertheless, in 1662, a young attractive redhead named Isobel Gowdie made an astonishing confession to the elders of her local kirk in Lochloy, near Auldearne in Morayshire. Bored by her marriage to a dull farmer, Gowdie admitted to having sex with the Devil. She had been initiated into Satanism at a Sabbat one night in Auldearne Church 15 years earlier. A large black hairy figure had read a diabolical liturgy from a black book. She was required to renounce Christ. Then, the Devil had sucked blood from her shoulder. A few nights later, she attended a meeting where the Devil had had sex with her and 12 other women. At later meetings, two children were sacrificed in the Devil's name and their bodies and blood were used in satanic rites. There were similar instances in England's North American colonies. In 1648, in New England, Mary Johnson admitted consorting with the Devil and murdering a child.

In the 18th century, Britain was scandalized by the satanic goings-on among the aristocracy. They occurred at Sir Francis Dashwood's infamous Hell-Fire Club, which he began in 1721

Sir Francis Dashwood.

while still in his teens. Although he said he remained a committed Christian throughout his life, Dashwood claimed to have used the Black Mass to invoke the Devil in the form of a black cat or a goat-like figure. Despite the condemnation of George I, Dashwood continued his activities. In 1728, he set off to 'fornicate his way across Europe'. In Rome, he attended the ceremonial scourging of Christ in the Sistine Chapel on Good Friday. During the ceremony, Dashwood pulled a real whip out from under this coat, cried: '*Il Diavolo*' and viciously lashed the congregation. He was ejected from the chapel and expelled from Italy.

Dashwood's Hell-Fire Club was by no means the only satanic organization in 18th-century England. Young Bucks amused themselves at The Banditti, The Blasters and The Sons of Midnight. These clubs emulated the French obsession with devil-worship and debauchery. There were at least three Hell-Fire Clubs in London and three more in Scotland. They all offered excessive quantities of alcohol, drugs and free sex.

Dashwood's club was undoubtedly the most exclusive, though. Members included Frederick, Prince of Wales, the Earl of Bute who went on to become prime minister, the Earl of Sandwich, MP John Wilkes, poet Charles Churchill, novelist Lawrence Sterne, satirist George Selwyn, at least one Oxford professor and the Archbishop of Canterbury's son, Thomas Potter. Dashwood himself rose to be Chancellor of the Exchequer in Bute's government. One distinguished visitor was Benjamin Franklin.

Meetings were initially held in The George and Vulture in George Yard in London. A naked girl spreadeagled on the bar-room table was used as an altar. A communion wafer was pushed up her vagina and the sacrificial wine was drunk from her navel and, when the Black Mass was over, there was an orgy.

SATANIC TEMPLE

When Dashwood married in 1745, his Hell-Fire Club curtailed its activities. But in 1753, it started up again, this time at Medmenham Abbey, near West Wycombe in Buckinghamshire. A complete satanic temple was excavated in the chalk caves there.

Members were now called 'monks' and wore red habits. The caves were hung with inverted crosses and pagan idols. One resembled a bird with its head turned around, so that its phallus-shaped beak protruded from its back. Women would ride this, in preparation for the mass orgies that would follow. Monks also had individual cells, where they could perform private rituals. Prostitutes dressed as nuns were shipped in from London for rites and orgies. Virgins were much in demand. Counterfeiting virginity was a growth industry at the time, though some of the women used were mere girls.

There are some indications that the rites performed in the Hell-Fire caves may have included sacrifices, possibly human. But all the records of the club were burned by Paul Whitehead, the man who actually ran the club, shortly before he died in 1774. Dashwood turned the Buckinghamshire militia out for his funeral and his heart was placed in a mausoleum built over the caves. It was said to have been 'as black in death as in life'.

Satanism went underground after the death of Dashwood in 1781. But two books published in France in the 1890s by Karl Huysman, a veteran of the French Sûreté, claimed that devil worship was rife from Paris to Hong Kong.

There were theories that the Jack the Ripper murders were the work of a Satanist. One suspect was the newspaper reporter, Roslyn D'Onston. A failed doctor and drug addict, he was said to have killed the women to give his career a fillip. In 1890, he became involved with Mabel Collins, the editor of *Lucifer*, the magazine of the Theosophical Society, a cult that sought to unite religion and science, and was founded by proven fraudster Madame Blavatsky. He later went into business with Baroness Vittoria Cremers, who revealed in the 1920s that she had found neckties caked with dried blood in D'Onston's room. She said that he had told her that they belonged to Jack the Ripper. These eventually found their way into the hands of Aleister Crowley, who claimed that D'Onston was indeed the Ripper and had performed his ritual murders in an attempt to become invisible.

NEW AGE OF SATAN

During much of the first half of the 20th century, there was enough tangible evil in the world to make Satanism surplus to requirements. But in the 1960s, it made something of a comeback. Throughout the British Isles, there were reports of graves being disturbed and magical symbols being painted on the walls of churches. In Ayrshire, Scotland, in 1964, a minister reported finding in a disused 17th-century church a partially burnt Bible, an inverted cross and a smashed chalice. And, in the small town of Helikon in Switzerland, a group calling themselves the Seekers of Mercy was broken up after a young girl in their care died in mysterious circumstances. An investigation revealed that the cult's 'church' boasted black candles and a fully equipped torture chamber. The dead girl had been sexually assaulted and brutally whipped while tied to an inverted cross.

Then, on 30 April 1966 – Walpurgisnacht – the First Church of Satan was established in San Francisco. Its founder was former circus artist and animal trainer, Anton Szandor LaVey. In the early 1960s, he quit the circus to work as a conjurer and hypnotist. Slowly, his interest in magic grew and he set up a circle of students studying the black arts. His satanic beliefs were very much in the Crowley mould.

'There is a demon inside man and it must be exercised not exorcized – channelled into ritual hatred,' he said.

LaVey claimed that satanic ages lasted 1,458 years. The last one, where God was on top and the Satan was cast down, started in AD 508. Consequently, the new satanic age began in 1966. This time, Satan would be on top. LaVey proclaimed 1966 'Year One, Anno Satanas'.

LaVey caught the mood of the time. He claimed that

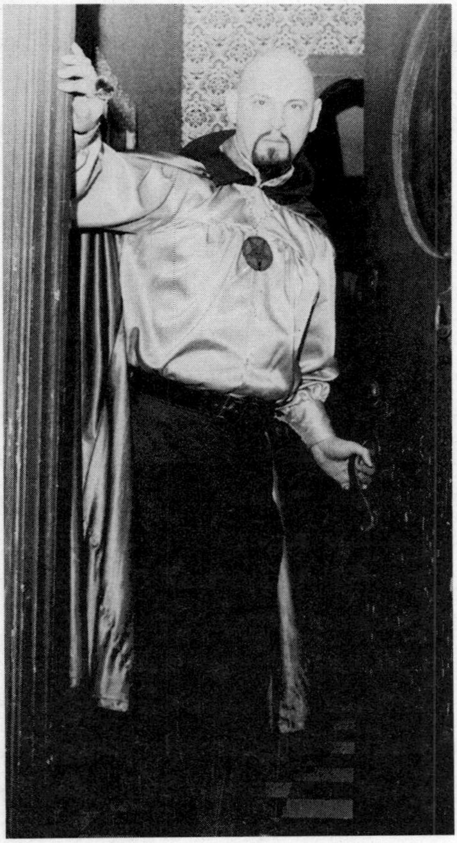

Anton LaVey.

Christianity has brought restraint, mortification, self-denial, discipline and conformity. Instead, Satanism offered indulgence, vitality and gratification. Sins, he argued, were really virtues when they brought physical and emotional pleasure. Within five years, he claimed 10,000 disciples worldwide. His church was recognized as a legitimate religion, with resulting tax-free status. He also produced two books, *The Satanic Bible* and *The Satanic Rituals*. These works have been cited at almost as many murder trials as Crowley's *Magick In Theory and Practice*.

The First Church of Satan attracted a lot of devotees in California because of LaVey's unashamed showmanship. He called himself the Black Pope, dressed all in black, shaved his head and grew a goatee beard. His home in San Francisco was in the middle of a block with empty lots on either side. The only things that grew in the barren garden were weeds. The curtains were black and never opened. A human skeleton hung at the end of the hallway. The living room was full of stuffed animals, including a fully grown wolf and a raven. His wife claimed to be a fully fledged witch and her hair hung a full three feet below her shoulders.

LaVey would use a pantomime devil-suit for his ceremonies, complete with horn and tail, and he would be greeted with the cry: 'Hail Satan.' His congregation would also be masked and robed in theatrical style. There was the obligatory nudity. A naked woman draped across the altar was, of course, de rigueur.

LaVey took Satanism to the people. He choreographed show-stopping satanic extravaganzas featuring topless dancers from seedy San Francisco bars. One of them was called Susan Atkins. She played a blood-sucking vampire in LaVey's 'Witches' Sabbath', a satanic revue performed at Gigi's nightclub in North Beach. She went on to become a leading member of Charles Manson's 'Family'. Convicted of murder, she died in prison.

The Black Pope revelled in his celebrity and boasted Sammy Davis Junior and veteran actor, Keenan Wynn, among his followers. Another member of his congregation was Jayne Mansfield. But her lawyer, Sam Brody, was very much against her involvement, fearing that it would hurt her public image. On 29 July 1970, Mansfield and Brody were driving in San Francisco, when a truck crashed into their car, killing them both. LaVey claimed to have had prior knowledge. He said that he had put a curse on Brody and warned Mansfield not to ride in a car with him. This was dismissed as tacky opportunism, but it helped put LaVey and the First Church of Satan in the public eye.

LaVey was employed as an adviser on the film Rosemary's Baby and had a walk-on part as the Devil himself. He was also technical director of the movie The Devil's Rain, starring John Travolta. This show-biz sell-out alienated some of his more committed followers. And when he started selling posts in the higher echelons of the church to his Hollywood friends, his followers split.

THE TEMPLE OF SET

US Army Officer Michael Aquino led one breakaway group and founded the rival Temple of Set, which was also recognized as a legitimate church by the IRS. The Temple of Set claims that it aims to teach 'responsible and ethical knowledge of the Black Arts' and to become 'the pre-eminent repository of the wisdom of the "left-hand path"'.

Aquino claimed to be a follower, not of Satan, but the ancient Egyptian god Set. He, too, rushed into print with The Book of the Coming Forth by Night, which again propounded the Crowleyan view that Satan was within man and must be released. Despite the more secretive and intellectual approach of his satanic church, Aquino also courted theatricality. He modelled himself on Damien Thorn from the Omen movies. While it is easy to dismiss him as a harmless crank, Aquino had top security clearance from the US Army. He served on the World Affairs Council and worked at NATO. This became a worry when it was rumoured that he had recruited at least 12 members of Army Intelligence into the Temple of Set. A police report noted that Aquino had worked in the Army's psychological warfare department and, when the Army tried to dismiss him because of his involvement with Satanism, he sued for discrimination, arguing that his right to freedom of religion was guaranteed by the First Amendment to the Constitution. He won. Later, he was promoted to lieutenant colonel, even though his increasingly fascist leanings were disturbing members of his own satanic organization.

Other spin-off cults created by the collapse of the First Church of Satan included the Temple of Baal, who claim in their advertising to be a 'spiritual organization dedicated to dominance, conquest, murder and slavery'. Another, the Warlords of Satan, are said to crave 'nothing less than to turn human beings into prey'.

In May 1970, 18-year-old Patricia Hall – also known as Inca Angelique – was arrested with three male drifters for the rape and cat-o'-nine-tails flogging of a teenage girl in a wax museum's hall of mirrors on Bourbon Street in New Orleans. She threatened to turn the arresting officers into frogs and claimed to have been baptized by LaVey in San Francisco. LaVey denied all knowledge of her. She was later extradited to Florida, where she was convicted of stabbing a 66-year-old man.

Throughout the 1970s and 1980s, there was a series of murders by confused young men, usually under the influence of drugs, who claimed Satanism as their inspiration. Many of them had begun their interest in the occult by reading LaVey's *The Satanic Bible*.

Middle-aged Man Looking for Sex

In Britain, Satanism did not die out with Aleister Crowley. In December 1995, self-styled Satanist John Kilminster came up in court for drug possession. This was embarrassing because he had been trying to keep his worship of Lucifer and his orgiastic rituals from his wife.

Northampton furniture-maker, chess champion and pillar of the local Conservative association, Kilminster had founded the English Church of Satan by putting an ad in the local paper. Their first meeting was held in a nearby Little Chef. Kilminster kindly provided new recruits with, among other things, a do-it-yourself werewolf kit.

The membership largely comprised middle-aged men interested in the possibility of free sex. Fortunately, a number of women signed up too. Rituals were held in Kilminster's workshop, made over with black drapes, black candles, burning incense and pentagrams. Kilminster would lie in a coffin, while the other Satanists pranced around naked under their black cloaks, awaiting his resurrection. The evening would end with 'a celebration of lust'.

In court, the bald, bearded Kilminster admitted to having sex with two cult members. He had also pursued one ex-cult member with whom he was besotted. Her cult name was Shiva and she claimed that Kilminster had spiked her drink with methadone to make her more open to his advances. Other cult members were given harmless aphrodisiacs.

CHAPTER 22:

THE PROCESS CHURCH

The Process Church of the Final Judgement was the brainchild of Robert DeGrimston Moore, aka 'The Christ of Carnaby Street' or 'The Teacher'. Born in Shanghai in 1935, he was educated at Winchester and studied architecture at Regent Street Polytechnic in London. While a student, he became a Scientologist. By 1962, DeGrimston had become a senior member and ranking officer of the Church of Scientology in the UK. Just as L. Ron Hubbard claimed to have studied personally under Crowley, so DeGrimston claimed to have studied in person under Hubbard.

At the Church's London headquarters in Fitzroy Street, DeGrimston met Mary Ann MacLean – 'The Oracle'. She was born in Glasgow in 1931. She had spent time in reform school and had briefly been engaged to the boxer, Sugar Ray Robinson. But when she met DeGrimston, she was working as a nightclub hostess on the fringes of the social circle that included Christine Keeler and Mandy Rice-Davis. One of her boyfriends was the society osteopath, Dr Stephen Ward, who was the only man to stand trial as a result of the Profumo scandal. One of Ward's many interests was a deep and enduring fascination with the occult.

DeGrimston and MacLean set up an informal group, who practised what they called compulsion therapy. This attempted to rid participants of all manner of compulsive behaviour by examining the complex reasons behind it. By 1963, the group's ideas began to deviate from those of Scientology, so DeGrimston, MacLean and their followers left the Church and set up on their own. They established the Process Church of the Final Judgement, which believed in both God and Lucifer.

IN SEARCH OF THE BEAUTIFUL PEOPLE

The Process Church preached a particularly broad interpretation of the concept of free will. The Jews, they argued, had chosen to be exterminated in the Nazi gas chambers during the Holocaust. People born disabled had chosen this course in a past life. These weird ultra-libertarian ideas struck a chord in the London of the 1960s. Beatniks and bikers flocked to the new religion, but the Process Church put most of its effort into recruiting the beautiful people – the wealthy and well connected who would supply the Church with funds and introduce its philosophy to the highest levels of society.

By March 1966, Process had enough money to lease a huge mansion in Balfour Place, Mayfair. DeGrimston, MacLean and 25 other cult members moved in. Each brought an Alsatian dog. In June, 18 members of Process went on a six-week holiday in the Bahamas. They moved on to Mexico, where DeGrimston leased a large piece of land at Xtul, a beach area on the Yucatan peninsula. There, Process members began practising the sex-and-satanism rites perfected by Aleister Crowley.

Back in London, DeGrimston was determined to bring his new theology to a wider audience. He threw Balfour Place open to the public, opened an occult bookshop and began producing a magazine expounding his philosophy. He tried to recruit the new young pop glitterati – the Beatles and the Rolling Stones – with some success. Mick Jagger's girlfriend, Marianne Faithfull, appeared on the front cover of the first issue of *Process* magazine.

DeGrimston also began to turn out books, explaining Process's creed in more detail. His first book, *As It Is*, was published in 1967. In it, DeGrimston laid out a clear, if perverse, philosophical line. Christ said: 'Love your enemies.' Christ's enemy was Satan, so Christ should love Satan and anyone who followed Christ should love Satan, too. This love would eventually break down the schism between Christ and Satan, good and evil. On the Day of Judgement, DeGrimston said, Christ and Satan would be reconciled. Christ would do the judging and Satan would execute Christ's judgements. Anyone who understood this simple truth should help bring about the reconciliation between Christ and Satan and hasten the Day of Judgement. Naturally, DeGrimston knew how to do this. In his second book, *Jehovah on War*, he wrote simply: 'Thou shalt kill.'

DeGrimston believed that a spree of motiveless killings would herald the Final Judgement. After all, the Book of Revelations said that the Battle of Armageddon would precede the Day of Judgement. But DeGrimston did not think that the human sacrifices that Crowley claimed to have made were enough. He preached that life should be one long murderous ritual.

In the summer of 1967, the cult moved to San Francisco and set up in the centre of hippie counterculture, Haight-Ashbury. Their headquarters were at 407 Cole Street. Just two blocks down the street, at number 636, there lived the ex-con and drifter named Charles Manson.

Later, the US wing of the Process Church moved to South Cochrane Street in Los Angeles. Manson followed. There, Hell's Angels and drug addicts from Sunset Strip, as well as minor pop singers and movie actors, became willing converts. Process tried to hook up with the First Church of Satan, but Anton LaVey dismissed DeGrimston and his followers as 'kooks'.

A meeting of the Process Church.

DRESSED FOR CHURCH

In the late-1960s, when everyone was wearing every colour of the rainbow, Process members stood out. They wore black suits, with black jumpers and black capes. The satanic Goat of Mendes was embroidered in red on the back of their capes. They also wore silver crucifixes around their necks. Half of them wore them inverted in the satanic manner. Another symbol of the Process Church was four 'P's joined at the foot like the arms of a swastika.

The Church was divided into three factions, which, DeGrimston said, would re-unite on the Day of Judgement. New members were free to choose which road they followed. One group followed Christ. They were strait-laced and puritanical. The second followed Lucifer. They enjoyed sex, drugs and rock'n'roll, and the other pleasures of the flesh. The third followed Satan. They believed in blood sacrifice and violence.

Process magazine gave equal space to the three factions. Issue four was devoted to sex. In it, the Christian faction argued that sex was a defilement. It was degrading and humiliating to the participants. Worse, the coupling of two human beings excluded God.

The followers of Lucifer called for cult members to:

'Wash away all pointless guilt, all worthless fear, all futile shame... all embarrassment and the crippling bonds of self-restraint... [when talking of naked women on mortuary slabs] you feel the atmosphere of death as you stroke the woman and then lie upon her.

'Priests in midnight garb, the congregation, men and women unclothed except for blood-red masks upon their faces stand silent for the presence of their Lord and Master Satan... A naked girl, fair-haired and in the very prime of youth, lies like a human sacrifice upon the altar... sink down in the decadence of excessive self-indulgence. Let no so-called sin, perversion or depravity escape your searching senses; partake of all of them to overflowing... There is nothing else now, with the end of man so near. There is no dialectic but death.'

Even though the Process Church seemed to treat the three factions even-handedly, the whole of DeGrimston's philosophy skewed towards the satanic. On the cover of the 'Sex' issue of *Process* magazine, there was a naked girl, spreadeagled on an altar. She is surrounded by hooded worshippers and above her is an inverted cross.

The fifth issue of *Process* magazine was the 'Fear' issue. In it, DeGrimston told cult members that 'by seeking out fear in living experience, we become fear itself'. No doubt, these words were taken to heart by Charles Manson who, by this time, had joined the Process Church.

CHARLES MANSON'S WEIRD RAMBLINGS

Whichever faction recruits joined, they were expected to spend some time in satanic worship. After all, blood rituals and sacrifices were a good way to maintain a hold over members.

The Process Church was highly structured. It had six levels – acolyte, initiate, messenger, prophet, priest and master. DeGrimston referred to the cult as 'The Family'. Members were assigned temple names. There were brothers, sister and fathers – but, strangely, no mothers.

The sixth issue of *Process* magazine was the 'Death' issue. Charles Manson, who had just formed his own 'Family', contributed an article. It was rambling and incoherent and revealed Manson's growing obsession with death. There can be little doubt that the teachings of DeGrimston helped him along his path to murder.

During his time in California, DeGrimston published his third great work of cult philosophy, *Satan on War*. In it, he wrote: 'Release the fiend that lies dormant within you, for he is strong and ruthless and his power is far beyond the bounds of human frailty.'

These words could have been written for Manson.

Soon afterwards, the Process Church broke up, largely because many of the original members from London had gone to the US on 90-day tourist visas, which they had long outstayed. Some went back to England. Others went underground. New branches of the Process Church were set up in Chicago, Dallas, New Orleans, Toronto and Cambridge, Massachusetts. DeGrimston and MacLean headed for New York and established a branch on Corelia Street in Greenwich Village. But the Boston branch was by far the most successful. It recruited through a soup kitchen it ran for the homeless. Several members of rock bands joined and the Church had its own show on a local radio station.

Although the Process Church pulled out of California, its followers did not. A large number of dead dogs were found in the area around Santa Cruz, just south of San Francisco. Most were Alsatians. They had been beheaded, mutilated, skinned and, often, drained of their blood.

MURDER CAPITAL OF THE WORLD

By the early 1970s, District Attorney Peter Chang described Santa Cruz as the 'murder capital of the world'. Co-ed killer Ed Kemper, family slayer John Linley Frazier and serial murderer Herbert Mullin were all active in the area at the time.

On 13 July 1970, 22-year-old Stanley Dean Baker, a lumberjack from Wyoming, was stopped by the California Highway Patrol near the Big Sur on suspicion of being a hit-and-run driver. When the registration plates of the vehicle failed to check out, the police searched Baker and his companion, Harry A. Stoop. In Baker's pocket, they found a well-thumbed copy of Anton LaVey's *Satanic Bible* and a finger. When the patrolman asked him to explain himself, Baker said, with masterly understatement: 'I have a problem. I am a cannibal.'

The car, it turned out, belonged to James Schlosser. Schlosser was a social worker from Montana who had picked up Baker hitchhiking outside Livingston, Montana. They camped on

Yellow River at the foot of a hill called, appropriately enough, Devil's Slide. That night, there was a thunderstorm. Awoken by the lightning, Baker said that he was overwhelmed by a cannibalistic compulsion, which had gripped him since he had received electrical burns in a car accident when he was a teenager. He killed the sleeping Schlosser, cut his heart out and

Stanley Dean Baker.

ate it in ritual fashion. Then he stole his car and took a finger along with him in case he got peckish later.

When Baker was strip-searched, it was discovered that his body was covered in occult tattoos. Baker claimed to be a practising Satanist and a member of a blood-drinking cult in Wyoming that was an off-shoot of the Process Church. They sacrificed dogs during their ceremonies and drank their blood. The group, he said, had a moveable carved wooden altar, a special sacrificial knife with six blades and a portable crematorium to dispose of unwanted remains. This was confirmed by another member of the cult. The cult called itself the Four P Movement – or Four Pi for short. This was an obvious reference to the symbol of the Process Church. Its leader, Baker said, was a wealthy doctor or business executive living in Los Angeles. He was known as the Grand Chingon, but his description fitted neither DeGrimston nor Manson. By that time, DeGrimston had left LA and Manson was in jail.

During his trial, Baker was linked to the murder of 40-year-old Robert Salem, an internationally known lamp designer in San Francisco. The victim's throat had been slashed and his ears cut off. The killers had written 'Satan Saves' on the wall of his apartment. Next to it was a crude drawing of a crucified man and the word 'Zodiac'. On Salem's stomach was carved the circle and crosswire that became the symbol of the Zodiac killer, a serial murderer who may have been responsible for as many as 40 murders in the Bay area in the 1970s. He was never caught.

Baker was never charged with the murder of Robert Salem. But for the killing of Schlosser, he was sentenced to life. At Deer Lodge Prison, he would crouch in his cell and howl like a werewolf. He was transferred to a maximum-security prison in Illinois where he became a model prisoner. In 1976, he applied to join the First Church of Satan but was refused admission.

CHAPTER 23:

ANOTHER FAMILY

There was another sinister Family in Australia. It was founded by Anne Hamilton-Byrne, who claimed to be the reincarnation of Jesus Christ. She obtained children by false pretences, changed their names to hers, dressed them alike and bleached their pudding-bowl hair peroxide blond like the children in *The Village of the Damned*. She also dosed them with LSD and other psychoactive drugs and taught them that they were to inherit the Earth after a forthcoming apocalypse.

Hamilton-Byrne was born Evelyn Edwards in the town of Sale, 100 miles (160 km) from Melbourne, Victoria, in 1921. She was one of seven children and spent time in Melbourne's Old Brighton Orphanage, just as her mother, a paranoid schizophrenic, spent 27 years in mental hospitals and died in one. Of her father Ralph, a World War I veteran, the orphanage's records merely note: 'Whereabouts unknown.'

Among the stories Evelyn told was that her mother was a medium and psychic who could communicate with the dead. She was also a direct descendant of the French royal family and a member of the Scottish Hamilton clan, whose name Evelyn later adopted. Even more fancifully, her father was an inventor and a close friend of Lawrence of Arabia, and her childhood home was 'a grand mansion with massive grounds'.

At the start of World War II, her father joined up again, stating his religion as Methodist. When he was invalided out in 1944, he was listed as a 'spiritualist'. Even so Evelyn maintained that he was a Buddhist. After the war, she claimed that her parents had gone to India to seek enlightenment at an ashram founded by Nobel Prize-winning poet Rabindranath Tagore, though he had died in 1941. She also claimed that her father was a friend of the British millionaire and philanthropist, Lord Nuffield, while her mother had a Tibetan guru and could travel outside her body.

FATAL CAR CRASH

In 1941, she married RAF officer Lionel 'Don' Harris. They had a daughter named Judith, who later called herself Natasha and was estranged. But after Lionel died in a car accident in 1955, Evelyn started calling herself Anne Hamilton. They were adopting a child at the time, but his death put paid to that. In her grief, she claimed to have had a spiritual awakening.

Anne then studied yoga, training with Margrit Segesman, a Swiss woman who had 'lived in Indian ashrams and followed a Tibetan guru… [and] claimed to have lived in an Indian cave for five years'. After three months, Segesman asked her to leave after she put a spell on a fellow student.

But her studies continued, By the early 1960s, Anne was conversant with Theosophy, Anthroposophy, G. I. Gurdjieff's *Fourth Way* and works by several spiritual teachers.

She taught Hatha Yoga, adding eclectic spiritual teachings to her classes, which mixed Hindu and Christian ideas with elements of the occult, like consulting astrologers and ouija boards. Her clientele was mostly wealthy middle-aged women, who were bored and unfulfilled. This paid for her frequent face-lifts, liposuction treatments and the blond wigs that ensured she appeared ten to 15 years younger than her actual age.

The formal founding of The Family occurred in 1962, when she met Raynor Carey Johnson, the Oxford-educated Master of Queen's College, University of Melbourne. He wrote books about the paranormal and the spiritual world beyond the material.

In 1962, she began an affair with Johnson's college gardener, a former South African naval officer named Michael Riley. She had impressed him with her prescience regarding the trip he and his wife Mary planned to India in the summer of 1962–3. Anne warned him that Mary would fall ill. The trip, to visit the ashrams of Vinoba Bhave at Santiniketan and Swami Pratyagatmananda at Calcutta, was cut short due to Mary's severe illness, a 'proof' that led Johnson and his family to commit to Anne in 1963. In a ritual involving the consumption of hallucinogenic mushrooms, Johnson, his wife, their daughter Maureen and four others recognized Anne as Christ and became the first members of what was then called the Great White Brotherhood of Initiates

Anne Hamilton Byrne in 1993.

and Masters. In 1965, Anne married Riley and went to live with him in the Dandenong Ranges outside Melbourne.

The next important recruit was Dr Howard Whitaker, who was experimenting with LSD at the clinic in Newhaven. This became a fertile recruiting ground for The Family. Two psychiatrists, Harry Bethune and John Mackay, and Newhaven's owner, Joy Vilimek, joined. When Mrs Vilimek died in 1969, the clinic passed into the control of a tax-exempt, non-profit-making foundation, with Anne Hamilton-Byrne being joint trustee and executor.

By that time, Anne had separated from Michael Riley and had met Bill Byrne. They quickly became involved. His wife May was unwillingly committed to Newhaven for treatment and she and Bill divorced.

Initiates accepted Anne's proclamation that humanity was in its final karmic cycle, after which there would be no further reincarnation. They accepted her as Christ, who would take on their sins, paying their 'karmic debt'. In return, she demanded total obedience and that they call her 'the Master'.

One devotee explained that the living master Anne Hamilton, was 'the very centre and soul and substance of the way of salvation laid down by the supreme father… without the love and help of the living master, no soul could ever be liberated from the material world. Sect members believed that Anne Hamilton could stop the endless reincarnations they were locked in.'

Members were obliged 'to do only what [they think] the master will approve. Then essentially it is the master acting, not the disciple… I went through a period where I would have died for Anne… Under these mind-expanding drugs, one was able to regress through one's life and back into past lives. This was clearing… clearing out things of the past. You had to go to Anne to get the clearing.'

UPPER-CLASS SECT

Membership of The Family was secret and only for the elect. Whitaker and Johnson were in Anne's inner circle; they introduced her to lawyers, teachers, doctors and other affluent professional people. At its zenith, 150–200 members gathered there several times per week to take LSD and listen to Anne preach. She would appear in blue or white robes, surrounded by blue light as Handel's *Largo* played, the air thick with incense, and take a seat on a throne-like chair. By the early 1970s, members gave a majority of their income to Anne, so that she and Bill became wealthy.

DARKER TURN

Things took a darker turn between 1971 and 1975, when Anne acquired 14 children and infants. Some were provided by Family members, others by irregular adoption procedures arranged by social workers, doctors and lawyers under her influence. Their surnames were changed to Hamilton – later Hamilton-Byrne after she married William Byrne in 1978 – by deed poll or by forging birth certificates. Dressed identically with uniform blond hair, the children were told they were Anne and Bill's biological children, while other Family members were told they were the result of a breeding programme.

Anne had a habit of wearing maternity smocks and claiming to be pregnant until well past childbearing age, and in fact after undergoing a hysterectomy in the mid-1970s. The women who looked after them were referred to as 'aunties'.

These children were held in seclusion in Kai Lama, near the town of Eildon, Victoria. They were allowed no contact with the outside world and were disciplined with savage beatings and starvation diets. Co-operation was ensured by the administration of a range of psychiatric drugs.

At puberty, they underwent an initiation where they were dosed with LSD and left in a dark room, which caused some psychological damage. The children were further indoctrinated during visits to gurus in the US and India. Anne's power over The Family and over the world of 'facts', demonstrated her ability to alter reality at will.

THE POLICE ARE CALLED

One girl was not having it. At the age of 17, Sarah Hamilton-Byrne became troublesome and rebellious. When she was expelled, she came to the attention of a private detective investigating the sect and discovered that she was not really Anne Hamilton-Byrne's child. They went to the police.

In 1987, Kai Lama was raided and the children were taken into care. Some of the aunties provided information about the adoption scam but were convicted of fraudulently obtaining money from the Department of Social Security. The Family's solicitor confessed to forging birth records.

Anne Hamilton-Byrne and her husband remained beyond the reach of Australian law in the US. But in 1993, they were arrested by the FBI and extradited to Australia. They were charged with conspiracy to defraud and perjury after falsely registering the births of three children as their own. They pleaded guilty to the lesser charge and were fined $5,000 (£3,900) each. They also paid compensation to victims in civil suits.

Bill Hamilton-Byrne died in 2004. Anne succumbed to dementia and died in 2019. Under the name Sarah Moore, the rebellious adopted daughter who had pulled the plug on The Family published *Unseen, Unheard, Unknown*, her account of life in the cult, in 1995. The documentary, *The Family*, was shown at the Melbourne International Film Festival in 2016.

CHAPTER 24:

SYNANON

College drop-out and former sales executive from Ohio, Charles E. 'Chuck' Dederich spent the best part of two decades roaming the US, a barely functioning alcoholic. He settled in Southern California, where his second wife persuaded him to join Alcoholics Anonymous. This got him off the booze, but she divorced him anyway, so Dederich started experimenting with LSD. AA was not equipped to handle that form of substance abuse.

In 1958, using his $33 (£25) county relief cheque, Dederich rented a storefront in Ocean Park and tacked up a sign, 'TLC', for the Tender Loving Care club. The following year, it was renamed Synanon, supposedly combining 'syn' ('together') and 'anon' ('unknown'), and began offering help to drug-users.

Its motto was 'Today is the first day of the rest of your life'. That's what Dederich told those joining his programme. Then, he left them to go cold turkey. The treatment centred on 'The Game', a form of group therapy devised by Dederich. People sat in a circle and took their frustrations out on each other – often by shouting. It was confrontational and abusive. What you said did not even have to be true. Sessions lasted up to 48 hours. It was, Dederich admitted later, a form of brainwashing.

As numbers swelled, Synanon moved into a large brick

building and those on the programme were required to live in. However, the residents of upmarket Santa Monica were not happy about having a drug rehab clinic in their neighbourhood. In 1961, Dederich spent just under a month in jail for zoning violations and operating a hospital without a licence. But in the eyes of Synanites, he was a martyr and this apparent persecution made them a more cohesive group.

THE BEST GUEST LIST

All things psychological were trendy in this era, the 1960s, and the Synanon house became a trendy hang-out for celebrities. With recovering jazz musicians in residence, they held the coolest parties. Guest speakers in 1963 alone included *Twilight Zone* creator Rod Serling, legendary sci-fi author Ray Bradbury and the original host of the *Tonight Show*, Steve Allen. Other visitors included Leonard Nimoy, Jane Fonda, Charlton Heston, Milton Berle, counterculture drug guru Tim Leary, architect and futurist Buckminster Fuller and labour activist Cesar Chavez.

Synanon even got the endorsement of politicians. In 1962, Senator Thomas Dodd from Connecticut said: 'There is indeed a miracle on the beach at Santa Monica.' Jerry Brown, who became Governor of California for the first time in 1975, visited with his father in the mid-1960s.

Dederich was claiming miraculous recovery rates of anything from 80 to 100 per cent. However, he declined government funding as this would have required some kind of independent verification through drug tests, for example.

To fund the programme, non-addicts were allowed to join. Synanon boasted 823 members by 1967 and moved into Club Casa del Mar, a fashionable beachfront hotel that opened in 1926 and had closed down after being used by the US Navy to house enlisted men during World War II. Restored, it has since been re-opened as an upmarket hotel.

When film director George Lucas needed a large group of people with shaven heads for the filming of his 1971 science-fiction movie *THX 1138*, he found that most actresses were reluctant to cut off their hair, and so he hired some of his extras from Synanon where devotees were happy to shave their heads. Robert Altman also hired members of Synanon to be extras for the gambling scenes in his 1974 movie, *California Split*.

The cult had already had its own movie in 1965. Called *Get Off My Back*, it was made by Columbia Pictures and starred Chuck Connors and Eartha Kitt, with Edmond O'Brien as Chuck Dederich. It was filmed on location in Santa Monica with the full co-operation of Synanon. Then in 1981, Bob Dylan mentioned Synanon in his song 'Lenny Bruce' on the album *Shot of Love*.

TOO MUCH FREEDOM

By 1968, a new type of Synanon membership was on offer – the Lifestyler. These members were allowed to have jobs outside Synanon, provided they handed over most of their income. With the money, Dederich bought property as far away as Detroit to set up new branches of the sect.

Dederich soon decided that it was a mistake to let the Lifestylers have free access to the outside world. Most of them were forced to leave, while those who sold their homes and moved in full time were allowed to stay. Drug addiction needed a lifetime cure that could only be provided by Synanon. Besides, Dederich claimed he was starting a utopian revolution. 'This is the kind of revolution that moved the world from Judaism to Catholicism to Protestantism to Synanism,' he said. 'This is a total revolution game.'

Children were to be brought up communally and were taken

from their parents at six to nine months. At first, their parents were only to see them once a week, then not at all. Some baulked at that and began to leave. Good riddance, Dederich said, they had not shown sufficient commitment to the cause. Their choice for members was made clear – Synanon or family.

For those that stayed the rule was simple. They had to do what Dederich did. If he took LSD, so, too, did they. He gave up smoking; they had to, too. Dederich then decided he did not want children around at all. Pregnant women were forced to get abortions, while men had to have vasectomies – except Dederich himself, of course. And when his wife Betty died, other couples had to split up.

As Synanon had given up running its drug-rehab programme, it could no longer claim to be a not-for-profit organization. Its business interests were bringing in millions

A Synanon wedding festival, 1972.

of dollars, though. So Synanon became a religion to maintain its tax-exempt status.

BITTEN BY A RATTLESNAKE

Dederich became paranoid and discipline was tightened. He ensured spies and suspects were severely beaten. Juvenile delinquents sent to Synanon by the authorities were physically abused for insubordination. And in case the outside world was hostile, in 1978, Synanon spent $200,000 (£155,000) on firearms.

That year, things began to fall apart. Former member, Phil Ryan, took legal action to reclaim his daughter. Two men from the cult beat him senseless in his driveway. He was in a coma for a week.

Attorney Paul Morantz, who had successfully represented a young woman held against her will by the cult, opened his mailbox and was bitten by a rattlesnake, whose rattle had been removed to keep it quiet. He was rushed to hospital and two members of the cult were charged with attempted murder.

A search of Synanon properties unearthed tapes where Dederich ordered the killing of Morantz and he was charged with conspiracy to murder. All three pleaded *nolo contendere* – no contest. While the other two went to jail, Dederich was put on probation after doctors testified that he was ill and would die in prison. As part of the deal, he had to step down as head of Synanon.

With its reputation in tatters, members left in droves. The IRS removed its tax-exempt status in 1991 and demanded $17 million (£14.5m) in back-taxes. Synanon went bankrupt and was dissolved. Charles E. Dederich died in Visalia, California in 1997.

CHAPTER 25:

EARLY CHRISTIAN CULTS

By the 12th century, the Catholic Church was in a mess. Services were conducted in Latin, which few of the congregation could understand. Most people were illiterate and could not read the Bible for themselves. But they could see that the Church was corrupt. Many clergymen lived openly with their mistresses as ecclesiastical marriage had recently been banned. They lived a life of luxury, while the congregation they were supposed to serve lived in poverty and squalor, while those who had money could buy indulgences to remit punishment for their sins.

In 1176, a wealthy French merchant called Peter Waldo decided to clean things up. It was a project bound to end in disaster. While the Pope gave him a special dispensation to preach, he also had to obtain a licence from his local bishop. However, as the Bishop of Lyon was one of the fat cats Waldo wanted to denounce, the licence was refused and, in 1184, Waldo and his followers were excommunicated and exiled from Lyon.

The Waldensians took a vow of poverty and became evangelical ascetics. On the road, they became more radical over the years. They rejected ideas of purgatory, transubstantiation, invocation, excommunication, confession, absolution, penance, the sale of indulgences and relics. They only celebrated baptism, marriage and the Eucharist once a year on the Thursday before Easter. They translated the Bible into French and – heresy of heresies – allowed women into the ministry.

Pope Innocent III offered the Waldensians the chance to return to the Church, and many did, taking the name 'Poor Catholics'. When that did not work, the Church resorted to persecution. Waldensians were imprisoned and burned as heretics. This was okay: while you might burn their body, you would be saving their immortal soul. Waldensian cells survived in remote settlements in the Alps, however. By the 16th century, there were still enough of them to form an alliance with their natural heirs, the Calvinists, as the Reformation got under way.

THE POPE'S PUNISHMENT

The persecution of the Waldensians largely came about because a more heretical cult had sprung up. In the 12th century, with the Crusades in full swing, travel to east and west increased enormously and ideas long suppressed in Europe began to surface again. Among them was Manichaeanism, a form of dualism propounded by the Iranian prophet, Mani.

This took hold in and around the city of Albi in south-west France, before spreading to Italy, Spain and Flanders. The cult's followers were called *Cathari*, Greek for 'pure ones', or Cathars. They took Zoroastrian dualism to its extremes. As the material world existed on the dark, evil side of the universe, Jesus Christ, who existed on the good side, could not have been born into it. He could not have died in it either, hence the cross had no significance. As the trappings of the Church existed in the material world too, the Cathars could not be doing with any of those.

The human soul belonged on the good side of the universe, but it was trapped in the body on the bad side. So Cathars were against marriage, sex, eating meat and drinking wine or anything that brought comfort or pleasure. Cheese, eggs and milk were also condemned as they were all by-products of sexual intercourse. While the laity were not required to hold too fast to this, complete abstinence was required of the *Perfecti* who formed the inner circle of the Church.

Fearing persecution, the Cathars kept their faith secret. But eventually their heresy came to the ears of the Pope. He sent Cistercian monks to convert them. This met with little success and they were mocked in the streets of Toulouse. Pope Innocent III sent an envoy to Count Raymond VI of Toulouse, who controlled the Cathar regions of southern France. When his envoy was assassinated, the Pope ordered the Albigensian Crusade, the first crusade in Europe.

In 1208, 20,000 knights under Simon de Montfort attacked the town of Béziers. When soldiers asked the papal legate Arnaud, Abbot of Cîteaux, how they could distinguish between Cathars and good Catholics, Arnaud replied: 'Kill them all; God will know his own.' They did.

Despite the slaughter of the entire population of Béziers, the Cathars fought on for another 40 years. Death holds little fear for those who believe that the world is an evil place. Many Cathars performed sanctified suicide through fasting. Given the choice between converting to Catholicism or burning, *Perfecti* chose martyrdom.

The Cathars' last stronghold was the fortress of Montségur in the Pyrenees. Thought to harbour Christian treasure including the Holy Grail, it was besieged by 10,000 men. After a ten-month siege, the Cathars finally surrendered. In March 1244, 244 men and women walked out of the fortress singing, straight into the massive funeral pyres prepared for them. No treasure was found.

CHAPTER 26:

THE SKOPTSY

If you value your body parts, it is best not to join the Skoptsy. They were an offshoot of the Khlysty, a flagellant sect in Russia that boasted Grigori Rasputin as a member. To avoid the sin of lust, men would castrate themselves, partially or completely, while women would have their breasts removed and sometimes underwent female genital mutilation. While only male castration is mentioned in the Bible, the Skoptsy saw human genitals as the mark of Cain. Adam and Eve were said to have the halves of the forbidden fruit grafted on to their bodies in the form of testicles and breasts. The removal of these, therefore, restored the Skoptsy to the pristine state before Original Sin.

It began in 1771, when a peasant named Andrei Ivanov was convicted of having persuaded 13 others to castrate themselves. While he was flogged and exiled to Siberia, his assistant, Kondraty Selivanov, escaped after 20 years.

In 1797, he presented himself to Tsar Paul I at St Petersburg. He told the Tsar that he was the Son of God who had been reincarnated in the person of Peter III, Paul's father who had been overthrown and assassinated in 1762. Tsar Paul was not impressed and Selivanov was imprisoned in a madhouse.

Released under Paul's successor, Alexander I, in 1802, he lived for

18 years in the home of a follower in St Petersburg. Selivanov now claimed the title 'God of Gods and King of Kings' and said he had secured the salvation of believers through a self-inflicted mutilation. Calling themselves God's Lambs or White Doves and maintaining that they were fulfilling Christ's counsel of perfection as given in The Gospel According to Matthew where Jesus said: 'I say to you that everyone who looks at a woman lustfully has already committed adultery with her in his heart. If your right eye causes you to sin, pluck it out and throw it away; it is better that you lose one of your members than that your whole body is thrown into hell. And if your right hand causes you to sin, cut it off and throw it away...'

Later, when asked whether a man should marry, Jesus replied: 'All men cannot receive this... save they to whom it is given. For there are some eunuchs, which were so born from their mother's womb: and there are some eunuchs, which were made eunuchs of men: and there be eunuchs, which have made themselves eunuchs for the kingdom of heaven's sake. He that is able to receive it, let him receive it.'

BAPTISM OF FIRE

The Skoptsy believed that Jesus had been castrated – which was why he never married. And the washing of his disciples' feet was seen as a symbolic, if not actual, castration of the apostles.

Self-castration was performed in stages. First, the testicles were removed. This was called the 'lesser seal'. Then the penis would be cut off in the 'greater seal'. The process was called the 'baptism of fire'. The aim was not to make the human race extinct, but rather to perfect the individual. In some cases, the pectoral muscles were cut into. The shoulders, back and legs were sometimes mutilated, too. This was done, apparently, so that angel wings could sprout.

The earliest female mutilations were recorded in 1815. Usually, only the breasts were amputated. In the ceremony, the left breast of a girl of 15 or 16 was severed in a warm bath. Afterwards, the raw flesh was cut into small pieces and eaten. Both breasts were often cut off and sometimes the outer parts of the female genitalia.

The Skoptsy did not condemn marriage and sex. Recruits were allowed to have one child – and those who had fled to Romania to escape persecution, two – before initiation. They had to swear a strict oath of secrecy. Meetings were held late at night in cellars. Women dressed in white. Men wore long white shirts with a girdle and baggy white trousers. Both either wore white stockings or went barefoot. Their ceremonies included hymn-singing, addresses and ecstatic dancing lasting until dawn.

When army officers and upper-class men also castrated themselves, the Tsar stepped in. In 1820, Selivanov was arrested again and shut up in a monastery where he died in 1832, aged 99.

However, Skoptsism did not die out. Nobles, military and naval officers, civil servants, priests and merchants continued to join its ranks, though not all of them mutilated themselves. Between 1847 and 1866, 515 male and 240 female adherents were sent to Siberia. In 1872, there were Skoptsy trials all over Russia. Nevertheless, two years later, the sect still numbered at least 5,444, including 1,465 women, though of these only 703 men and 160 women had mutilated themselves.

An unsuccessful attempt was made to kill off the sect by ridicule. Male Skoptsy were dressed up in women's clothes with fools' caps on and paraded through the villages. When that failed, a further 130 Skoptsy were sentenced to transportation in 1876. To escape prosecution, some emigrated, usually to Romania, where they were known as Lipovans. Those eunuchs that remained in Russia were compelled to register. Nevertheless, Skoptsism continued to flourish until it was stamped out in the Soviet Union by Joseph Stalin.

CHAPTER 27:

RAËLISM

If you're going to start a cult you need a good back story. And the back story behind Raëlism is whackier than most. In 1973, 27-year-old former pop singer and motor-sports journalist, Claude Vorilhon, said he was driving in central France. Fancying some fresh air, he stopped his car, parked up and took a stroll around the craters of a nearby extinct volcano called Puy de Lassolas. There, he said he saw a UFO land, and a small French-speaking alien got out. Over the course of several meetings, the alien explained that scientists from its planet had used the Earth as a laboratory, where they created life. Vorilhon, the alien explained, had been picked to explain this to the people of the world. He was to change his name to 'Raël' – which meant 'messenger' – and was to be their ambassador on Earth.

STRANGE ENCOUNTER

Born in Vichy in 1946, Claude Vorilhon ran away from boarding school at the age of 15 and hitchhiked to Paris, where he found himself living on the streets. To make money, he started singing in cabaret and making records, although his ambition was to be a racing driver and, when he started his own magazine, *Autopop*, he found that manufacturers would lend him sports cars to test-drive on the racing circuit.

He had been doing this for three years when he had his encounter with the alien who said he was an 'Elohim'. This, he explained, meant: 'Those who came from the sky', but had been mistranslated as 'God' in the Bible. They met for six consecutive days, so that the alien could dictate the content of the book Raël would eventually publish as *Le Livre Qui Dit La Verité* (*The Book Which Tells the Truth*). Between sessions, Raël said, he was entertained by six 'voluptuous and bewitching' female robots.

To promote the book, Raël left journalism, appeared on television and gave public talks. He then founded MADECH, which stood for the '*Mouvement pour l'Accueil Des Elohim, Créateurs de l'Humanité*' (Movement for Welcoming the Elohim, Creators of Humanity), as well as '*Moise À Devancé Elie et le Christ*' (*Moses Preceded Elijah and the Christ* [*sic*]. This became the International Raëlian Movement.

In 1975, Raël said he was taken to the Elohim's home planet, where he met Buddha, Moses, Jesus and Mohammed, who were 40 of the Elohim-human hybrids that became prophets. He, of course, became the 40th. There, he was also shown the factory where biological robots were made and heard about the need for 'geniocracy': government by those who are clever and compassionate.

WORD SPREADS

The Raëlian Movement spread worldwide, soon claiming a following of some 90,000 members. Vorilhon moved the headquarters to Canada, where UFOland was established as the first embassy for extra-terrestrials. Later on, the Raëlians moved to Las Vegas, where, it was thought, people were more open-minded to whacky ideas.

The Raëlian Movement advocated the use of sex-positive (rather than anti-sex) feminism, the distribution of condoms and other methods of birth control, masturbation, meditation, genetically modified organisms and human cloning, which they saw as the first step towards immortality. The plan was to clone the most beautiful members of the movement first. These chosen few appeared in the October 2004 issue of *Playboy* magazine. The women posed for a feature called 'The Raël World', coyly subtitled 'Prepare for a close encounter of the nude kind'. It pointed out that nudity wasn't incompatible with spirituality, apparently. 'Let us not forget that the philosophy of the Raëlian is the only one that embraces sexual freedom and nudity,' a press release said. 'Three members of the Raëlians, the religious sect that believes life on Earth was started by space aliens, give a whole new meaning to the idea of heavenly bodies in the October issue of *Playboy* magazine.'

Along with Clonaid – an organization set up for research into cloning – Raël founded Clitaid, a non-profit organization, whose aim is to build a 'pleasure hospital' in Burkina Faso to offer medical services for the physical restoration and rehabilitation

Claude Vorilhon.

of victims of female genital mutilation. He fundraised for the cause at the AVN Adult Entertainment Expo in Las Vegas. In addition, Raël said he was interested in cloning, so that Hitler could be brought back to life to be punished and also to make sure that suicide bombers would not escape justice.

Within the movement, there were women-only groups. One of these, the Order of Angels, prioritized sexual gratification and offered their wombs and eggs for cloning experiments. Female supporters were also called upon to train as consorts for the aliens and Raël, their prophet on Earth. They were regularly replaced by younger women. Another female-only group, Raël's Girls, held seminars that began with 'sensual meditation' and became increasingly sexually adventurous.

INITIATION CEREMONY

Another part of Raëlian belief was the baptism ritual: a guide member would place water upon the forehead of the individual being baptized, and this would give the guide a good understanding of the individual's 'cellular chromosomic plan', which would be judged by the Elohim in the final hour. Baptisms were performed on four specific days a year – 6 August, the anniversary of the bombing of Hiroshima; 13 December, when Raël's first encounter with the Elohim took place; 7 October, when he visited the Elohim's home planet; and the first Sunday in April, when Adam and Eve were created.

According to Raël, our solar system, galaxy and universe are tiny particles within the atomic structure of some immense organic being. Within the atoms in the cells of our bodies, he believed there were minute planetary systems and galaxies inhabited by intelligent creatures like ourselves. The existence of the Elohim proved this, he said.

Raël has found himself in trouble with several governments for following his advocacy of cloning and his emphasis on pleasure in sexual education for children. He has also been accused of the existence of plagiarism in his numerous books.

He could not be accused of plagiarism when it came to the Bible. Apart from the fact that it was out of copyright, he had made substantial changes to it. According to Raël, the first verse of the Book of Genesis should read: 'In the beginning the Elohim created the heaven and the Earth.' The second verse – 'And the Spirit of the Elohim moved upon the face of the waters' – meant that extra-terrestrial reconnaissance flights had begun over the Earth, which was completely covered with water and thick mist.

'And the Elohim saw the light was good' apparently meant that the scientists had checked whether light from the Sun was harmful. After more tests, they terraformed a continent – 'Let the waters under the heaven be gathered together into one place, and let the dry land appear.' The vegetable cells were synthesized from chemicals which reproduced – 'Let the earth bring forth grass, the herb yielding seed, and the fruit tree yielding fruit after his kind, whose seed is in itself, upon the earth.'

CREATION MYTH

In the beginning, there had been a group of scientists who wanted to 'open the eyes' of humankind about their true origins. They were banished to exile on Earth as 'serpents'. The rest of the Elohim departed, leaving humans to their own devices. When the exiled 'serpent' Elohim then began interbreeding with humans, the other Elohim decided to end the experiment and sent nuclear missiles to destroy them. The exiled Elohim told Noah to build a spaceship to preserve what had been created by carrying single cells of the male and female of every species thousands of miles into space. The exploding nuclear missiles of the true Elohim then caused a great tidal wave – a flood – that killed every form of life left on the surface of the Earth.

Raëlism holds that the Tower of Babel was not a building but a space rocket, which the true Elohim destroyed, and those with the technical knowledge to build it were scattered across the Earth. However, some evil-doers congregated at Sodom and Gomorrah, which then had to be destroyed by atomic bombs. Then, to test that the remaining humans were sufficiently docile, Abraham was asked to sacrifice his son.

The story of Moses and the exodus from Egypt was explained in terms of the intervention of the Elohim. Eventually, Jesus was resurrected by way of a scientific cloning process. This, of course, could be construed as blasphemy.

The Raël Movement also ran into controversy over its symbol, which was originally a swastika inside a Star of David. This was modified: the swastika was bent into a 'swirling galaxy'. The official reason given by Raël was that the Elohim had requested this change in order to help the movement obtain permission from the Israeli government to build an extra-terrestrial embassy in Jerusalem. Despite the change, permission for this building project was still denied, and in 2007 the swastika returned as part of the movement's symbol, as, according to Raël, it was 'a symbol of peace for millions of Hindus and Buddhists and for the Raëlians as well, as it is their symbol of infinity in time, their symbol of eternity'.

Raëlists believe that humanity must find a way to harness new scientific and technological development for peaceful purposes. When this has been achieved, the Elohim will return to Earth to share their technology with humanity and establish a Utopia. Don't hold your breath. This could all take a while...

INDEX

PICTURE CREDITS

Alamy: 20, 38, 144, 151, 174, 178, 225

Getty Images: 13, 32, 51, 65, 66, 100, 110, 119, 133, 137, 141, 160, 187, 213, 221, 229, 236, 246

San Diego State University: 87, 92,

Shutterstock: 27, 167,

Topfoto: 73

Wikimedia Commons: 11, 22, 30, 42, 78, 84, 153, 172, 185, 194, 201, 204, 207, 209